The Feather Bender's
FLYTYING
TECHNIQUES

This book is dedicated to my father, Edward Ord Clarke, who died of a hard life shortly before my sixteenth birthday.
Like any great father, he taught me to fish.

When I was about eleven years old, I recall a day trip to Bakewell in Derbyshire. We stood side by side on the bank of the river Wye, spellbound, watching a fisherman casting in a way I'd never seen before. I asked my father what the man was doing. 'He's fly fishing; we'll have to try that one day,' he replied.
We ran out of time…

Dad, this book is yours.

The Feather Bender's

FLYTYING TECHNIQUES

A Comprehensive Guide to Classic and Modern Trout Flies

BARRY ORD CLARKE

Skyhorse Publishing

Skyhorse Publishing books may be purchased in bulk at special discounts for sales promotion, corporate gifts, fund-raising, or educational purposes. Special editions can also be created to specifications. For details, contact the Special Sales Department, Skyhorse Publishing, 307 West 36th Street, 11th Floor, New York, NY 10018 or info@skyhorsepublishing.com.

Skyhorse® and Skyhorse Publishing® are registered trademarks of Skyhorse Publishing, Inc.®, a Delaware corporation.

Visit our website at www.skyhorsepublishing.com.

10 9 8 7 6 5 4

Library of Congress Cataloging-in-Publication Data is available on file.

Cover design by Merlin Unwin Books
Cover photo credit: Barry Ord Clarke

Print ISBN: 978-1-5107-5150-7
Ebook ISBN: 978-1-5107-5151-4

Printed in China

CONTENTS

THE FLIES

FOREWORD
by Marc Petitjean

I first met Barry in 2009 on the river Trysil in Norway. I was drift-boat fishing this beautiful wild river while he was taking pictures in the magnificent scenery. We became good friends and a few years later we worked together on my book CDC. Barry's photographs made a great contribution to the book and I was proud to feature this great talent.

Now it's my turn to praise him as a fly tyer, a fisherman and a photographer. It's pretty rare to combine those three talents equally.

Barry was already a well-established professional photographer in England, long before moving to Norway and making fishing and flytying his living.

Barry is to flytying what a gifted multi-instrumentalist is to jazz: a man able to play the standards, to improvise or rearrange. Take for instance his CDC para-weld hackle: using the traditional para loop hackle as a starting point, he gives the parachute hackle a totally contemporary twist. Or his All Hackle Dry: with this pattern he makes a great innovation, mixing Japanese minimalism with a creative hackling technique.

In addition to his impeccable skills at the vice (he truly can tie every kind of fly), Barry shows a deep understanding of the materials, especially the natural ones, about which he speaks as both a nature lover and a hunter.

That's why you will learn a lot from this book in which he reveals so many useful tricks and tips, in both his words and pictures.

And as if that wasn't enough, Barry will also give you a "parallel" masterclass via his YouTube channel, The Feather Bender.

Barry Ord Clarke: a true artist and virtuoso at the vice.

Marc Petitjean

INTRODUCTION

My childhood years in the early 1960s were spent in industrial northern Lancashire, where I was as attracted to water as I am now. All my time was spent with a split cane rod on the local canals and millponds that drove the wheels of the world's largest cotton industry. Later in life, my chosen career as a photographer led me to London, where I was introduced to flytying. Unlike most fly fishermen, I started tying fully dressed salmon flies before I even started fly fishing. Having been fortunate enough to have had an "Arts and Crafts" art education, and a life-long fascination with birds and their plumage, flytying came naturally.

The nature of fly fishing, for most of us, is such that once you have taken the first step and learned to cast with a fly rod and eventually landed your first fish, you gain instant membership to a very special international brotherhood without cultural or social boundaries. We all become members of the family of fly fishermen.

Our enthusiasm and hunger for knowledge within our sport and its related subjects becomes a vocation. Whenever and wherever we meet, by the water on a day in high summer, or around a table on a cold winter's night, whether with old fishing friends or total strangers, we eagerly exchange experiences, techniques, and sometimes even precious tips. If you are new to our sport, you truly have something to look forward to. You may find the technical language barrier a little difficult to begin with—not to mention the Latin!—but it doesn't take long before you too are talking in tongues. No matter where you meet a member of this fishing family, you will always have something to talk about, with the conversation flowing easily from tackle, big fish, and destinations to, last but not least, flies and flytying.

The second step, and probably most natural progression from fly fishing, is to flytying. After the industrialization of the fishing hook, and the labor-intensive manufacture of fishing flies, the production has moved to countries with cheaper labor. The days are gone when fly fishermen tied flies out of financial necessity.

The move to the fly tyer's bench is motivated by sheer pleasure and, through flytying, the fly fisherman can open previously locked doors and enter a whole new world of their sport, customizing existing patterns to their own specific requirements, and in time designing their very own flies!

The first flies that a beginner attempts to tie are normally well-known patterns that have worked well for them. This is always a good place to start, as long as the patterns don't require especially difficult techniques or difficult-to-source materials. Frustration at an early stage can quickly lead to dejection and the danger that your flytying kit ends up in the attic, along with the windsurfing board and golf clubs.

On the other hand, if the beginner starts the flytying journey with a couple of highly fishable patterns that are technically easy and enjoyable to tie, these can be the stepping stones to more advanced and challenging patterns, via which the novice fly tyer will eventually be able to tie all the flies he or she requires, and more besides.

This book is aimed at all flytyers, from those with modest experience to more advanced skills, and my aim is to give tuition in certain important elementary techniques, and in particular to share some of my favorite contemporary twists on old techniques. Many of the flies in this book use my own techniques and patterns which I have developed over thirty-five years of tying.

When learning to tie a new pattern, the techniques, the knowledge of a material's potential and its limitations: these and many other considerations all have their place on the road to success. One of the key factors to this success is having available good tutorials. This book will give you the best detailed images available, for every step, from attaching the tying thread to the finished fly. All this is accompanied with a clear instructional text which will lead you through each of the patterns.

But what makes this book a first for flytying is that each pattern is also supported by a Quick Response code which instantly links you to my YouTube channel and the right video for each and every pattern here. Here you can see how I tie them, before you start to tie.

Another possible first: you can also send me a personal question if you are struggling, via the comments box on the video in question on my YouTube channel.

This is not just a book of fishing flies, although the patterns included will all catch fish: this is a book about mastering flytying techniques. Flytying has come a long way in the last decade or so. Many tyers are now taking the craft to another level and are spending more time at the vice than on the water. Like a child in a sweet shop, fly tyers love to look at flies and have a real appreciation for a perfect fly box, where the examples of each pattern are identical, all lined up like soldiers on a parade ground. With the help of this book, a good deal of practice and a pinch of patience, you can master proportions, uniformity and perfection. The only restriction on your flytying creativity will be the limits of your own imagination.

HOW TO USE THIS BOOK

I recommend that you start by scanning the QR code or using the link provided next to the dressing for each fly and watching the video, and familiarize yourself with the pattern. Here you can see me demonstrating any special procedures or techniques, and learn first-hand how I do it. **Full instructions –** *see* **page 251.** You can then turn to the book and follow the step-by-step instructions to tie at your own speed and leisure.

The book has been arranged in sections to give the reader the opportunity to locate the pattern or technique they are looking for with ease. I have not grouped the patterns alphabetically but by fly type (eg. mayflies, caddis flies, etc). For example, the section on mayflies has categories demonstrating mayfly nymphs, emergers, duns and spinners, all of which contain a multitude of techniques for tails, bodies, wings, and hackles, etc.

If you are fairly new to flytying, the opening chapters on materials and special techniques and tricks will familiarize you with some basics and help you get started. There are probably even a few things here for the seasoned fly tyer.

The index at the back of the book will tell you where to find particular patterns, techniques or materials. When you have located the page number for the desired technique, each pattern is listed with a recipe, recommended hook style, size, and materials. These are listed in the order that I use them in the book's step-by-step images and the accompanying video. This will help you plan each pattern and assemble your materials beforehand, for a more effective and enjoyable tying experience.

I hope that you, like me, are inspired.

Barry Ord Clarke, Skien, Norway, July 2019

TIPS AND TRICKS

Failing to prepare is preparing to fail

Save time by organizing your materials

When I started tying flies, all my tools, materials and hooks were all stored in a shoebox-sized plastic container. Thirty-five years later they now require a 50-square meter room solely dedicated to tying and photographing flies.

No matter how small or large your tying area is, try to give your materials a storage system that is easy to access, and easy to remember where things are. This dramatically reduces the time you waste searching for materials, which increases tying efficiency and enjoyment.

 Watch video:
youtu.be/pQFNGQzVpy0
A little tour of my tying room with Barry Ord Clarke

Prep your materials before tying

When you intend to tie a half dozen or more of the same pattern, prepare all the hooks and materials needed for the number to be tied. I count out the correct number of hooks needed, then place them in a small plastic container, then prep the materials. Select all the hackles in the correct size and prep these by stripping off the downy section and trimming the stem.

If you are using hair, cut all the bunches required and clean and stack: these can then be placed in a simple hair holder ready for use. If it is tinsel or floss, cut it all to the correct length, and so on . . . When you have prepped all the materials, clear an area on your tying bench and lay the hooks and materials out in the correct order to be used.

Proportions

The correct tying proportions for a good-looking pattern will always be a matter for debate. Try to develop a system for your favorite proportions for each pattern: this is not only important for prepping your materials but even more important for attaining the correct symmetry and balance, which after much practice will make each fly identical to the last.

I always have a 30cm ruler on my tying bench, placed between me and the vice for easy access. In this position you can quickly measure materials to the correct length, when both tying and prepping. This will not only improve your fly proportions, getting wing, hackle, and other materials to a uniform length, but it will also save you materials, by you cutting the correct length needed of tinsel or floss from a spool.

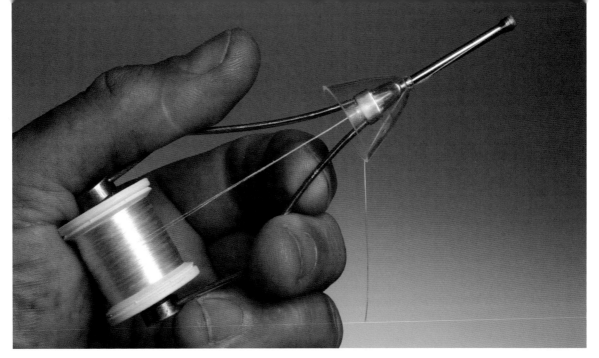

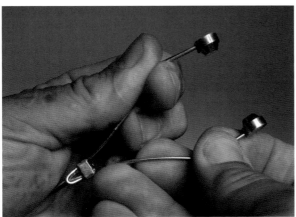

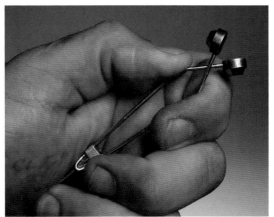

Adjust bobbin tension

This is probably the most overlooked element of tying that will help with every single pattern you tie! Over the past twenty-five years I have held hundreds of flytying courses and demos. In just about every single course I have students who have been tying with the bobbin tension so tight that they are bending the hook or breaking the thread every few winds! Or, on the other end of the scale, the tension is so slack that when released from their hand it un-spools and falls onto the table or the floor! What you need to achieve is a tension that has just a little resistance when you pull on the bobbin. If further tension is required, let's say when flaring deer hair, this can be applied by using the palm of your hand as a brake.

Many of the new, more expensive bobbins have a built-in tension adjustment screw or slide, but the more simple bobbin designs are easy to adjust if you know how.

Firstly hold your bobbin holder as shown in your left hand and draw off a little tying thread with your right hand. This way you can determine if the tension is too tight, or too slack.

If the tension is too tight, remove the bobbin from the holder and gently open the spigot arms, forcing them slowly apart (see left photo on page 13). Don't overdo this to start with, just a little at a time. Once you have done it, replace the bobbin and check the tension. Repeat until the correct tension is acquired.

If the tension on your bobbin is too little, remove the bobbin from the holder as before, and gently cross the spigot arms, forcing them slowly together (see right photo on page 13). Don't overdo this to start with, just a little at a time. Once you have done this, replace the bobbin and check the tension. Repeat until the correct tension is acquired.

Magic Head hackle guard

This is a simple homemade tool that helps tame hackles and hair when whip finishing. Buy a pack of large Petitjean Magic Heads. If you are not going to use these for tying streamers, split the price of a pack with a tying friend.

Thread one Magic Head over your bobbin holder as shown on page 13. They also make great thread retainers for keeping all your bobbins in check.

Once all the required deer hair has been spun and packed, you have to make a whip finish.

This can be difficult with all that hair flying around, so just slide the Magic Head up over the hook eye. This will hold all the hair out of the way, for a trouble-free whip finish.

Hackle pliers

The majority of flytying tools that are used on a regular basis become worn after long use. The small rubber sleeve around one of the jaws supplied when purchased becomes dry and eventually splits and rots. We have all experienced the common problem, when winding on a hackle: just at that critical moment the jaws slip, releasing the hackle stem, resulting in a good dose of frustration.

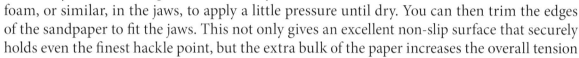

I solve this problem with some extra-fine glass paper and a couple of drops of super-glue. All you have to do is cut two small patches of sandpaper and glue them to the inside of the jaws.

Once they are attached, place a sheet of fly box foam, or similar, in the jaws, to apply a little pressure until dry. You can then trim the edges of the sandpaper to fit the jaws. This not only gives an excellent non-slip surface that securely holds even the finest hackle point, but the extra bulk of the paper increases the overall tension in the jaws, resulting in a tighter non-slip grip.

Watch Video:
youtu.be/nFHfAkiOvXU
Improving your hackle pliers with Barry Ord Clarke

Dubbing needle cleaner

A dubbing needle is a tool that I use on every single fly I tie. It's also the tool that is most often mislaid amongst the clutter of materials while tying. In order to avoid this I have at least five dubbing needles of various sizes, all placed in a foam block by my vice.

I can also recommend a dubbing needle with a long handle and short needle. This gives you a better grip, and so much more precision when applying varnish.

The acute point of a dubbing needle becomes easily clogged with a build-up of varnish and head cement which you have to scrape off with a hobby knife. If you use an empty plastic hook box, filled with wire wool or even a normal Brillo pad, the days of clogged dubbing needles are over.

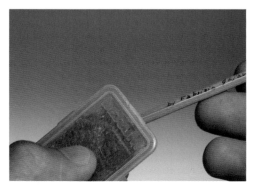

Once the box is packed tightly with wire wool and the lid securely in place, make a hole by pushing the point of your dubbing needle through the center top of the box and down into the wire wool.

Repeat this three or four times, without withdrawing your needle completely from the box. Your needle is clean, highly polished, and sharp.

Toothbrush

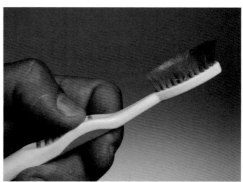

Once my toothbrush has foregone its usefulness in the bathroom, it is reincarnated in the flytying room as a dubbing brush.

This is one of those simple tying tools that I have been using for as long as I can remember: just the right size, but large enough and bright enough to be found anywhere amongst the clutter of your tying table. A large, easily-held handle and short stiff bristles make it excellent for a wide range of flytying tasks.

Hair clips and hair band spool retainers

These very inexpensive small hair ties are extremely useful, especially if you are tying large predator and saltwater flies. These little bands will hold materials in place thereby freeing up a hand to help with tying. You can store two or three of these bands on the main shaft of your vice for easy access.

They are also perfect for retaining spooled materials, keeping normally unruly tinsels, wires, and flosses in check.

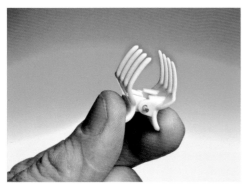

These small hair clips, costing only a couple of pounds for a packet of many, are extremely useful. They will hold the tying thread and materials out of the way, freeing up a hand to help with tying. You can store two or three of these clips on the main shaft of your vice for easy access.

Organize your tools

Over the years I have acquired many tools, but only use a handful on a daily basis. Keep your tying area free of these never- or seldom-used tools, making your tying bench tidier and more efficient.

Take a look at your tying bench and select all the tools that you use for just about every fly you tie: scissors, bobbin-holders, whip-finisher, hackle plier, etc, and put these to one side. Then put on the other side the tools that you use only occasionally. What you are left with should be tools that you can put away in a box to be retrieved for the very rare occasions when they are needed.

There are many tool caddies and racks available to help organize the essential tools at your vice, but if you use a little imagination you can find ingenious ways of storing your tools efficiently and creatively.

I probably have a larger selection and stock of hooks than the average fly tyer, but no matter how large or small your collection, keeping your hooks organized will help you locate the style and size that you require for each pattern with ease.

MATERIALS USED IN THIS BOOK

Antron yarn

A synthetic yarn that consists of parallel strands of trilobal Antron thread. Sold on a card in as many colors as it has applications. Great for wing cases, parachute posts, body silk...

CDC

CDC, short for Cul de Canard or Croupion de Canard, was first used as a flytying material in the 1920s in Switzerland. In more recent years the Swiss perfectionist Marc Petitjean has been responsible for popularizing the use of this material. All birds have these feathers, but the best for flytying come from ducks. The feathers are located around the gland that produces preening oil. This highly water-repellent oil is collected on these small feathers, and the bird uses the oil to dress and waterproof its plumage. Without preening oil, the bird would drown. The small CDC fibers catch tiny air bubbles that work on dry fly and emerger patterns. With weighted nymphs, the tiny bubbles resemble the gasses emanating from splits in the nymphal shuck when in transition. Besides its excellent floating properties, CDC is extremely aqua-dynamic, pulsating with life in the water. And a CDC hackle will collapse under air pressure while casting but, as soon as the cast ends, the hackle opens and falls perfectly back to its intended shape.

Coq de Leon

These are spade hackles from the roosters of rare breeds of domestic fowl that originate from the region of Leon in northern Spain.

Flor de Escoba

The feathers have remarkable coloration and, in the traditional Spanish patterns in which they are used, are not wound onto the hook as a normal hackle. Instead, bunches of the fibers are bound onto the hook and then splayed with the tying thread to obtain a radial hackle effect. The speckled plumage also make excellent tails and caddis wings. The feathers have become more easy to obtain in recent years as their popularity within flytying has risen. In their finest form the feathers have a stiffness and glasslike translucency that come from birds bred at high altitude on a soil which is rich in chalk. The quality of feather is also affected by the time of year they are harvested from the birds. The feathers come in two different types: Indio, which are solid and plain colored; and Pardo which are mottled.

The traditional names given to the Flor de Escoba colors are:

Indio

Negrisco (black); palometas (white); rubion (natural red); palteado (silver grey); acerado (ash grey); avellanado (brownish grey); perla (pearl grey); claro (light grey); oscura (dark grey).

Pardo

Flor de Escoba (dark background with reddish brown spots); sarrioso (light brown background with pale russet brown flecks); corona (fallow deer background with pale russet brown flecks); aconchado (conch shell); langareto (mottled in distinct yellowy lines); encendido (flushed with red); medio (medium-shaded and stippled); oscura (dark shade); crudo (immature indistinct mottling).

Roe deer hair

During the darkest, coldest months of the year with the shortest days, the roe deer adopts its thickest, most dense coat. With up to a meter or more snow on the ground for several months, and often with temperatures in double figures on the wrong side of zero, this is when the roe needs the extra insulation. This hair is thick and spongey when squeezed, with a good amount of underfur for extra insulation and a noticeably more fatty/waxy feel to the touch. The diameter of each individual hair has also increased, containing larger air cell honeycombing than at any other time of the year, creating optimal flaring of 90 degrees when compressed under the pressure of tying thread. This makes it perfect for spun deer hair flies. This late-season hair can be spun, packed, and clipped into almost any desired shape, so tightly that it doesn't resemble deer hair at all.

Hackle

Hackles traditionally arouse the greatest passion amongst fly tyers. Cock/rooster capes of particularly good or rare color and those with sufficiently short barb length to enable small dry flies to be tied have always been prized. In the 1960s and 70s it was a common complaint that good dry fly capes were scarce—to the extent that many of the "traditional" natural colors were virtually unobtainable. Dyeing and other methods such as blending two hackles were used to replicate difficult colors specified in old patterns.

Things have improved dramatically since then, due to the efforts of specialist breeders and modern techniques of fowl husbandry. Many traditional colors have reappeared in quality that far exceeds anything that was obtainable in the past. These developments come at a price however and the tyer will have to pay for top quality cock cape or saddle from the best-known American "genetic" hackle farms.

That special dry fly cape or saddle in a unique color is a tyer's most prized possession. There is a whole load of mystique that surrounds the hackle, without doubt the most used material in flytying. It has so many applications: tails, dry fly and streamer wings, quill bodies, feelers, palmered, parachute, paraloop, and traditional hackles, just to name a few.

An appreciation of quality hackle comes only with practice and viewing and handling many kinds and grades of hackle over time. Some of the most important points to look for are:

Color

This is usually the first consideration. The best capes have an even and uniform color that conforms to one of the traditional color designations. It is worth noting however that where a cape lacks uniformity of color or is of a "nondescript" color, it may still be of excellent quality in all other respects. Such capes are often less expensive and can be used either as they are, or for dyeing.

Condition

The healthiest and strongest birds produce the best-conditioned feathers. Dr Tom Whiting, owner of Whiting Farms, has said that when choosing birds for breeding he considers not only color and quality but also the character of the birds. No matter how good a color a bird has, if it is poor spirited it will not get a good deal in the pecking order, so its health and condition and therefore feather quality are unlikely to be the best. Such a bird rarely produces top quality hackle or makes a contribution to the bloodline.

The overt appearance of a cape is often a good first indicator of general condition. Birds in good health and condition seem to "glow" and the individual feathers are clean and springy. Poor condition often manifests itself in a dull, bedraggled appearance with thin spots, possibly indicating poor diet, infestation or disease.

Feather count

It is clearly desirable for a cape to have as many feathers of a useful size as possible. Some indication of feather density can be gained just from feeling between finger and thumb the thickness (depth) of a cape where the back of the cape starts to widen (the shoulder). Bending the cape at this point will "raise the hackles" so that they fan and stand proud from the skin and separate. Individual hackles can then be examined and some assessment made of the numbers and size distribution.

The best quality capes have high numbers of hackles with barbs short enough to tie the tiniest dry flies. These capes command the highest prices.

So if you are tying larger patterns it is clearly pointless buying expensive hackles in mostly size 22-28. Indeed if one is tying mainly size 10-16 flies, then a lower grade cape will not only be cheaper but may have better and more hackles in the size needed.

Usable hackle length

You should look closely at the characteristics of individual hackles. The best cock hackles furnish the highest barb count and density along the shaft (stem) and they provide the longest portion of "usable hackle." This portion is called the "sweet spot" and is where ideally all the barbs on each side of the shaft are of a uniform length. The hackle shaft, the backbone of the hackle, should also be fairly thin and flexible to allow easy bending for wrapping round the hook shank.

Hackle shafts that are too thin will break more easily and those that are thick will have little flexibility and be bulky when tied in. Hackle stems that are brittle—possibly through bird age or poor drying technique—are almost useless.

The best hackles have a long sweet spot and high barb density along the shaft, allowing more barbs to be wound onto the hook with minimum turns of hackle. The longest sweet spots to be found are on some of the super grades of saddle hackle. These are so long that many densely hackled flies can be tied from a single hackle.

Hare's mask

This refers to the mask and ears of the European brown hare. Individual masks range in color from pale tan to almost black. The texture and length varies from fine and soft in the underfur, which is an excellent dubbing, to long and stiff guard hairs which can be used for feelers and tail in many patterns. The ears are covered with short stiffer hairs without almost any under-fur. A mixture of hair from the ears and the mask makes one of the best buggy nymph dubbing available.

Mallard flank

The natural grey barred flank feathers from the mallard drake come in small, medium and large sizes. They can be used for all manner of tasks and patterns, from the wings of the smallest dry flies to large bait fish patterns. With careful dying you can also use them as a wood duck substitute. When purchasing, try to avoid mixed unsorted packs as you'll find that most of the material is unusable. Choose packs of feathers selected by size or a whole skin.

Marabou

These fluffy plumes originally came from the African marabou stork. But these birds have been strictly protected for many years and the acceptable substitute comes from the thighs of the domestic turkey. Turkey marabou is a favorite material for winging lures, streamers, and saltwater patterns. The individual fibers are very soft and mobile, producing a sinuous lively action under water. Marabou is also used extensively in imitative patterns such as dragon and damsel fly nymphs, leeches and worms.

Melt glue/hot glue

Melt glue is a material that requires practice. Once it is mastered, it can be put to use not only in developing new patterns but also as a substitute in existing ones. Melt glue guns come in various sizes from hobby to industrial. I find the hobby size not only the cheapest but also the easiest to use. Another advantage with the hobby gun is the amount of different glue that is available. The glue has a low melting temperature and is available in just about every color imaginable—and then some.

Moose body hair

The dark brown to jet black straight body hair ranges from medium to coarse in texture. It can be spun if an open clipped body is required, but it requires extreme thread pressure. This hair is stiff, with a large diameter at the base that tapers slowly to a fine tip.

It is extremely buoyant and between 2"-5" in length. It has many uses such as tails and wings of dry flies, as in the Wulff series. It can also be put to use as extremely realistic legs and feelers on nymphs and terrestrials. For the wing cases on Humpys or any other pattern where durability is a prime consideration, moose body hair is a first choice.

Moose mane

Moose mane is the longest hair, especially from an adult bull, and is located on the back of the neck of the animal. The mane hair can range from 3" to a huge 9" in length, but is not suitable for spinning. The color is a wonderful salt and pepper mix of white, grey, brown and jet black hairs, that have long been used for wrapping quill bodies on dry flies and nymphs.

I find the best moose mane hair for tying quill bodies is untreated, ie not washed or tanned, since these processes remove the natural waxy fats from the hair which reduces the suppleness, making it more difficult to wrap. Being fortunate enough to hunt moose myself, moose mane is always available to me, but for most tyers, shop-bought processed hair is the next best alternative.

A trick for regaining some of the suppleness is to soak individual hairs in warm water for 20 minutes or so before you use them. Tying in two hairs by the tips, one dark, one light in color, and wrapping them together creates great segmented bodies. If you tie regular or even double Humpys, this long hair is perfect for the wing cases and wings. The different colored hairs can also be woven to form exceptional nymph bodies.

Partridge

The grey partridge or English or Hungarian partridge as it is also known, is widely used in flytying. The speckled brown back and speckled grey breast feathers are used in many traditional patterns, both wet and dry. The barred and blotched and cinnamon quills from the wings and tail are also used to good effect for caddis wings.

Peacock herl

The eye tail-feather from the peacock provides us with the famous herl. Covered in iridescent green fibers it is used for wound bodies, butts, and wing cases in hundreds of patterns. For stripped herl patterns, the best herl to use is from just under the eye of the tail feather. These herls are stronger here than otherwise found on the tail.

Pheasant tail

The least expensive and most common pheasant tail used in flytying is from the ring neck pheasant. The best feathers come from the center of the tail of the cock pheasant. These long center tail feathers have the longest fibers and normally the best chevron-barred markings.

Polypropylene yarn

This is a smooth-textured synthetic yarn available in many colors, which is less dense than water, ie it floats. Polypropylene yarn is particularly suited to dry fly applications, such as wings, parachute posts, shuck cases, wing cases. Silicon-coated polypropylene yarn is even more water repellent than standard polypropylene.

UV resin and light

After the introduction a decade ago of Bug Bond, which was probably the first UV resin for flytying, there is now a multitude of UV activated resins available to the fly tyer. UV resin is a light-cured acrylic that is activated with the help of a UV torch. The greatest advantage of UV resin is that unlike epoxy there is no waiting time for drying. Excellent for coating bodies and heads of all manner of patterns. Available in various viscosities and colors. A great addition to any tying bench.

DYNEEMA
and TYING THREAD

The sheer number of spools of thread that I have accumulated over the years is mind-boggling! I have silk, nylon, polyester, kevlar, dacron... this list goes on! The tyer always looks for thread to suit the job in hand, in terms of diameter, 16/0 or 3/0, stretchability, flat or round profile, waxed or unwaxed, saltwater resistant, and not to mention color! I could go on and on...

Just over a decade ago I replaced the chaos of literally hundreds of spools with one single tying thread, in one color and one size! Is that possible, you may ask? Here are the pros and cons of Dyneema.

Dyneema, or GSP (gel-spun polyethylene), is a UHMwPE fiber, ultra-high molecular weight polyethylene. It is manufactured by means of a gel-spinning process which has more recently been adapted for fishing line. It combines extreme strength with incredible softness, and no stretch. In other words, it is stronger, weight-for-weight, than steel, and it's extremely lightweight so that build-up, turn for turn, is minimal on the hook shaft. The chemical makeup of Dyneema also means that it doesn't rot, it's resistant to most chemicals, saltwater and UV light.

Because its structure is made up of many extremely thin fibers, it can be spun in a clockwise direction and the fibers will then twist into a single super-strong 16/0 ultra-fine tying thread with a round profile. If you spin the thread in an anti-clockwise direction, the fibers will open up and the thread will acquire a flat profile, more like a floss silk.

These two attributes mean that this one single size of Dyneema works for both the smallest, #28 patterns, up to the largest saltwater hooks.

When the fibers are flat you can also split the thread and make a dubbing loop for spinning light materials, such as CDC, marabou and dubbing. But if you intend to spin heavier furs, such as rabbit, you need to double the thread and make a loop in a traditional manner. This makes a much stronger loop, better for gripping heavier materials with dense underfur. With the fibers open (flat), it also becomes a first-rate thread for spinning deer hair, but be warned, if you try to spin and flare deer hair with the thread twisted into a round profile, it will cut through the deer hair like a hot knife through butter!

When it comes to thread color, Dyneema and GSP tying thread is, as far as I am aware, only available in white or grey, the latter marketed as black. When unspooled, it is more opaque, but its fibers can be colored easily with waterproof or spirit-based felt pens. The advantages of this are many. You only need one color of tying thread, but of course you do need spirit-based felt markers in the colors required. This reduces not only the clutter of your tying station but also time taken in changing spools or bobbins. It also eliminates unnecessary build-up on underbodies through attaching and tying off other colors of threads and flosses.

When varnishing heads tied with Dyneema, on applying the varnish you will see that it is absorbed immediately into the fibers, resulting in a solid and extremely durable finish.

Working with Dyneema

Avoiding an uneven base for floss and tinsel underbodies

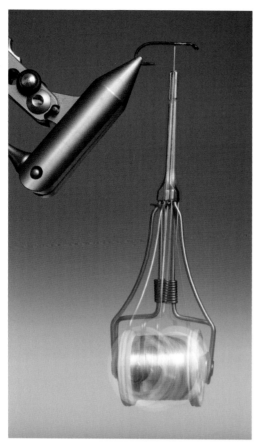

1. Once you have securely attached Dyneema to the hook shank, let your bobbin hang vertically. Grip the tube of the bobbin between your index finger and thumb and spin anti-clockwise and the fibers of the thread will open flat.

Take care not to over-spin the thread as this will re-twist the fibers into a negative round profile. If you are unsure, let you bobbin hang motionless and it will naturally unwind in the opposite direction.

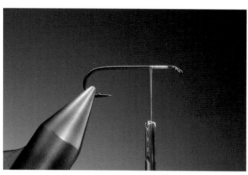

2. Now that your thread has a flat profile, you can start winding on the foundation. But remember that for every turn of flat thread made on the hook shank, the remaining thread from the hook to the bobbin will twist one turn in the negative, re-twisting the thread. To counter this, I spin the bobbin, just a little, after every eight to ten winds onto the hook shank to return it to its flat profile.

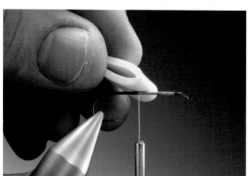

3. If a perfect tinsel or floss body is required, once the foundation of Dyneema is laid, carefully polish the thread with a piece of closed cell foam by rubbing it carefully back and forth along the hook shank. This will shove all the open fibers into any micro-gaps that have occurred during winding. The result is a perfect, flat, even underbody.

Coloring Dyneema

With your thread hanging, and holding the bobbin in one hand, color the thread with a spirit-based pen by running the felt tip back and forward along the length of tying thread required.

Please note that if you require a relatively large amount of thread colored, in other words more than the amount from the hook shank to the ceramic tube when the bobbin is hanging, it is best to color it a little at a time. If you pull off, say, 20cm or more thread from the bobbin and color it, and then wind it back onto the spool immediately, the color will penetrate into the remaining spooled Dyneema.

 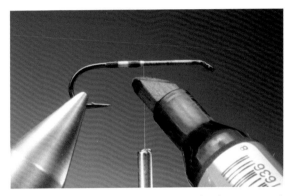

Once you have finished with the required color, you can carry on tying with the natural Dyneema, or color the next length required!

Splitting the Dyneema

If you need to make a dubbing loop, follow the instructions for spinning the thread anti-clockwise as in step 1. Once the thread is flat, take a preferably dark cylindrical object (I use a short section of a rod blank). While your bobbin is hanging, gently move the cylinder up and down along the tying thread and it will open flat against the cylinder. Take a dubbing needle and split the thread in the center.

Once split, open the loop, and hang one side over your vice. This will keep the loop open, while you prepare your materials for spinning.

As mentioned earlier, this method is only suitable for spinning light materials because the weight of the spinning bobbin holder gives insufficient tension in the twisted tying thread.

If you wish to spin heavier, more dense materials, make a traditional loop and use a heavier brass dubbing spinner. Also if you spin hair with a dense underfur or a heavy dubbing, wax the Dyneema loop before you insert your material. Because Dyneema has an extremely smooth profile, the wax increases purchase and stops the material slipping.

Strength

Stronger, weight-for-weight, than tensile steel, Dyneema is difficult to break when applying increasing tension evenly through the bobbin.

As you can see (*below*) a single strand of spun Dyneema has no problem bending a #4 streamer hook without breaking!

However, care should be taken. If by accident, while tying with Dyneema, you brush the hook point with the thread, some of the nano fibers will break, as with floss.

If you are lucky you can repair this with a little saliva, by just sticking the fibers back in place along the thread and winding onto the hook shank until you have passed the break. Or remove the thread and start again.

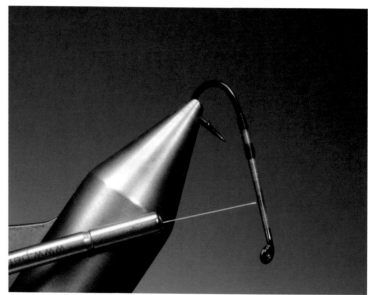

THE FLIES

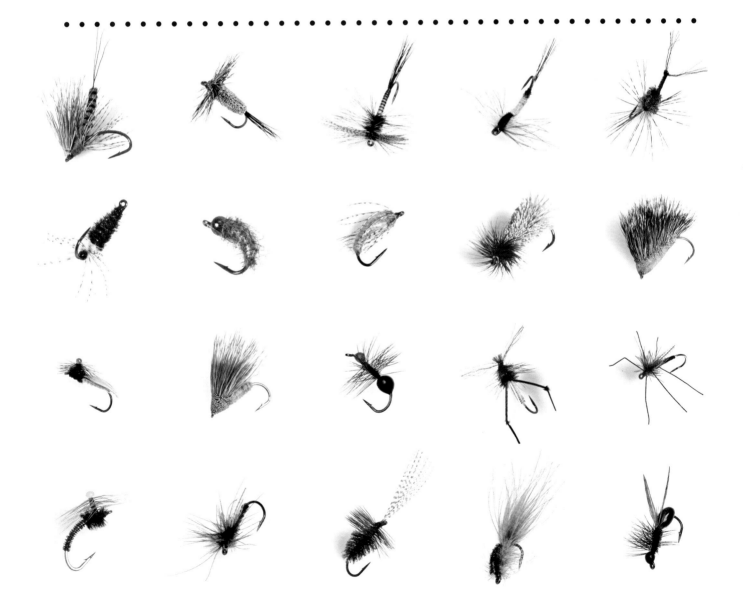

①

Gill Abdomen Mayfly Nymph

Larva Lace abdomen • Herl gills • Pheasant tail wing casing

This is an alternative technique for creating a segmented mayfly gilled abdomen effect, for nymphs.

Imitating gill-bodied mayfly nymphs has always been a challenge for the fly tyer. Many fishing patterns dismiss the gills altogether, whereas other super-realistic representations replicate them down to the smallest intricate detail. Although lots of fun to tie and admire, it is not advisable to spend several hours painstakingly tying a super-realistic pattern which can go wrong on the first cast!

Inbetween these two extremes is a huge playground of materials and techniques at the disposal of all fly tyers, to surmount these design challenges, especially for those fly tyers who are not afraid to think outside the box. This relates to all flytying, not just gill-bodied nymphs! Just because a material is designed or marketed for a single specific use, it doesn't mean that it won't lend itself to other applications or techniques. Be adventurous. Start by asking yourself a few questions:

• Does it float or sink?

• Will it melt?

• Does it stretch?

• Try twisting it!

By addressing these and other questions, you will become a better fly tyer. Acquiring an in-depth knowledge of your materials, their applications and limitations, will only broaden your skill as a craftsman and designer.

As with so many other successful trout patterns, the winning combination of pheasant tail and peacock herl is by choice and not by chance.

This pattern is relatively quick to tie, but still retains a semi-realistic feel to it. I can't emphasize enough how important good quality materials are for achieving the best results for good-looking flies.

It's fine with synthetics because they are identical in every possible way.

Although the materials used in this pattern are universal, it's worth taking a little time to source the best available.

Pheasant tail refers to the tail feathers of the ring neck pheasant from both cock and hen birds. And you will find that many shops sell not just center tail feathers, but feathers from the whole tail of both cock and hen mixed in a vase marked 'Pheasant tails'. What you should look for is the larger cock pheasant center tails. These have much longer fibers than any of the others found on the tail, and they make the best tails and legs on both nymphs and dry flies. Each individual fiber is also ribbed with a dense herl which, when wrapped, is ideal for bodies, thoraxes and wing cases.

You should also scrutinies not only the color on each individual tail feather, but also the markings, as no two feathers are identical. Most of the above also applies to peacock herl.

The Indian peafowl, or blue peacock as it is also known, is what fly tyers generally use, but it has recently been placed on the CITES list (Convention on International Trade in Endangered Species). This could mean that the main suppliers of peacock feathers worldwide, India and Pakistan, may no longer be able to legally export it. So dealers will have to rely on existing stock, or on domestically-bred birds.

This suggests that it will become more difficult to obtain in the future, but until then, while we can still purchase peacock plumage, do so wisely.

Try to avoid buying strung peacock herl, which is almost never good: you will search all day through the bunch to find a single strand that isn't broken or damaged. Look for whole peacock eye tops that have a full bodied herl, and a lustrous, iridescent sheen to them. These will totally change the quality of your flies.

TECHNIQUES MASTERED

- **Larva Lace gill-ribbed abdomen**
  I demonstrate a good method for preparing and tying with Larva Lace to make an even-tapered, segmented body.

- **Peacock herl gills**
  Precision positioning of the herl over each turn of Larva Lace in which the peacock herl is pulled down inbetween each segment to form the gills and protect the herl.

- **Pheasant tail wing case**
  Creating a double wing case of pheasant tail fibers to form the perfect profile of a mayfly nymph: broad at the abdomen and thin at the head.

Tying the Gill Abdomen Mayfly Nymph

THE DRESSING

Hook: Mustad S82 #8-14
Thread: Olive
Tail: Pheasant center tail fibers
Body: Larva lace & peacock herl
Wing case: Pheasant tail fibers
Thorax: Peacock herl
Legs: Pheasant tail fibers

WATCH THE VIDEO

youtu.be/TH7KNHmXx10

Gill Abdomen Mayfly technique with
Barry Ord Clarke

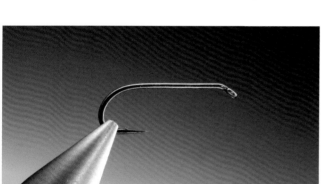

1 Secure your nymph hook in the vise, as shown, with the hook shank horizontal.

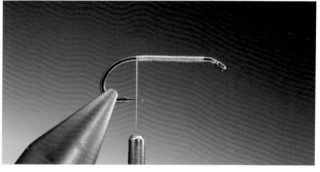

2 Run a fine foundation of tying thread along the hook shank to the bend.

3 Select a small bunch, about ten, of nicely marked center pheasant tail fibers for the tail. Tie these in about the same length as the hook shank.

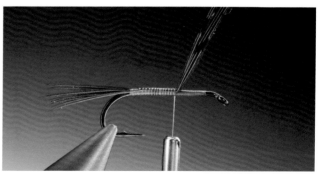

4 Secure these about two-thirds of the way up the hook shank, where the thorax begins.

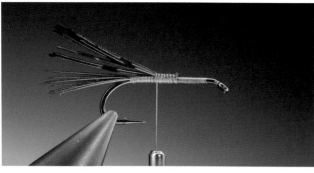

5 Now fold the fibers back towards the tail, and tie down about halfway so you can build up a tapered underbody.

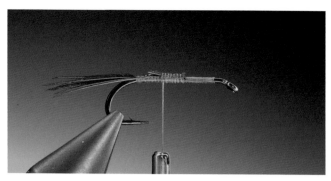

6 Carefully trim off the excess fibers at an angle.

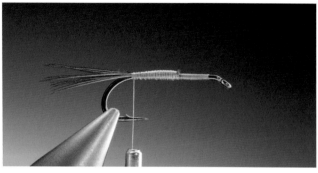

7 Before you start wrapping the underbody, spin your bobbin anti-clockwise, which will give your tying thread a flat profile. This will make for a smoother underbody.

8 Cut a length of clear Larva Lace. Melt one end with a lighter and pull it so it stretches and breaks. Take care not to burn the house down or your fingers! This should result in a super-fine taper for tying in.

9 At the tail base on the rear of the hook shank, tie in the fine tapered end of the Larva Lace, as shown.

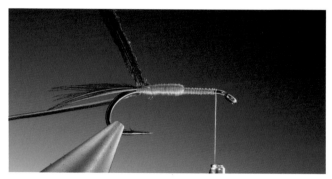

10 Select a peacock herl with nice long fibers and tie this in, just in front of the Larva Lace.

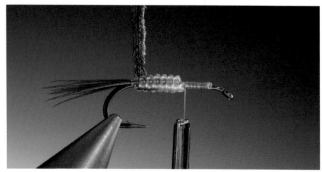

11 Stretch the Larva Lace for the first couple of turns and then slacken off as you wrap forward. This will make the Larva Lace thinner at the tail base and thicker towards the thorax, resulting in a well-tapered abdomen. Tie it off and trim away the excess.

12 Now carefully wrap the peacock herl, pulling it down inbetween each segment of Larva Lace. Secure with a few turns of tying thread at the thorax.

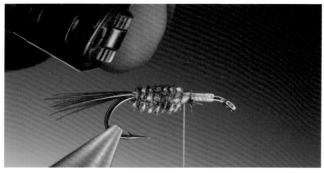

13 Not on the highest flame setting, using a lighter, carefully burn away the herl fibers on top of the abdomen.

14 The top of the abdomen should now look like this!

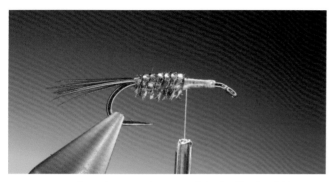

15 From the side view, the peacock herl gills should be visible on the underside of the abdomen.

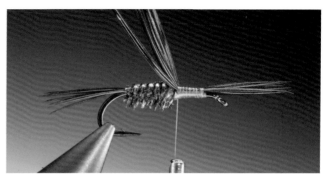

16 You will now need two small bunches of pheasant tail fibers, about seven fibers per bunch. Tie the first bunch in on your side of the thorax. Remember to leave enough (about a hook's length of the fibers) over the hook eye for the nymph's legs.

17 Now do the same with the second bunch of fibers on the other side of the thorax, as shown.

18 Select three large fired peacock herl and tie these in by the butt ends, close into the abdomen and wing case.

19 Holding all three peacock herls parallel and together, wrap them over the thorax. Tie off a little behind the hook eye as shown, leaving enough room for the head.

20 Push the pheasant tail tips back over each side of the thorax and secure with tying thread, finishing close to the thorax.

21 Keeping all the pheasant tail fibers parallel so they don't cross and weave over each other, fold them over the hook eye to form the wing case. Make two or three turns of tying thread as tight into the thorax as possible and make two turns under the fibers around the hook eye to secure it.

22 Cut away the remaining pheasant tail fibers and, starting at the hook eye, work your way back with turns of tying thread to secure the head.

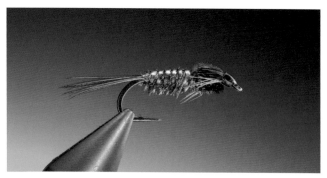

23 Make a couple of whip finishes, remove your tying thread and varnish.

24 The bird's eye view of your finished gilled mayfly nymph should hopefully look something like this!

Pheasant Tail Nymph

Pheasant tail body • Reverse wire ribbing • Herl thorax

The original pheasant tail nymph was created by legendary English fly tyer and fisherman Frank Sawyer around 1930. He designed the pheasant tail to imitate Baetis mayfly nymphs on the southern English river Avon, where he was riverkeeper. Sawyer's original pattern used only pheasant tail fibers and fine copper wire instead of normal tying thread, to give the pattern extra weight.

The modern variants of the PTN that we are familiar with, including the one illustrated on page 39, bear little resemblance to the original. Although this modern version is an excellent imitation of the swift swimming baetis nymphs, in larger sizes it also works as a generic nymph for blind fishing.

With only three materials and the tying thread needed for this pattern, it still helps to choose the right materials.

At first glance, one pheasant tail feather looks like any other pheasant tail feather—or does it? Take a look at a few cock pheasant tail feathers side by side, and you will see they are very different! Not only does the background color and shading on each tail differ immensely but the black chevrons vary from light to dark and from thin to thick.

But probably the most important factor is the fiber length. Normally the best marked feathers with the longest fiber length are found center top of the cock bird tail.

So remember when buying pheasant tails, don't just take the first one you see in the shop: look through them all and find the best for the flies you intend to tie. Examine the feather: is the tip dirty and worn? If so, it probably came from a domestically-bred bird. The best tail feathers are generally from wild birds. Check if the feather is clean and has a nice glossy sheen to it and that all the fibers are in place.

You should also avoid tail feathers with insect damage. This can easily be seen as a thin transparent line that runs 90 degrees from the feather stem through the fibers, where the insect has eaten the feather's barbules.

Below: At a glance, one pheasant tail feather looks like any other pheasant tail feather – or does it? As with all natural materials, no two are the same. The background color, markings, mottling, sheen and fiber length will be different on each and every feather. When buying pheasant tails, scrutinize these factors before making your purchase.

TECHNIQUES MASTERED

- **Pheasant tail body**
  Choosing and wrapping pheasant tail fibers to form a tail and perfect tapered nymph abdomen, all from a single bunch.

- **Reverse copper wire rib**
  How to position and wrap a fine wire rib in a reverse direction to the pheasant tail, not only for segmenting the abdomen but also for holding down and therefore strengthening the pheasant tail fibers.

- **Herl thorax**
  Increasing the thorax length with peacock herl to create a longer, more sleek overall nymph body profile.

Tying the Pheasant Tail Nymph

THE DRESSING

Hook: Mustad S82NP #8-18
Thread: Olive
Tail: Cock pheasant tail fibers
Abdomen: Cock pheasant tail fibers
Rib: Fine or medium copper wire
Thorax: Peacock herl
Wing case: Cock pheasant tail fibers
Legs: Cock pheasant tail fibers

WATCH THE VIDEO

youtu.be/IWsRFNoq5OQ
Tying the Pheasant Tail Nymph
with Barry Ord Clarke

1 Secure your nymph hook in the vise so that the hook shank is horizontal.

2 Attach your tying thread and run a foundation over the whole hook shank, until the thread hangs approximately vertically with the hook barb.

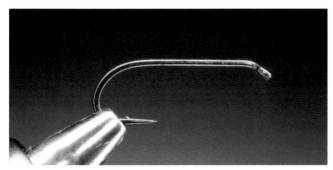

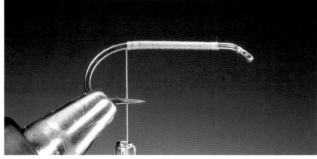

3 Firstly find a cock pheasant center tail feather with nice markings and long fibers. To get all the points of the pheasant tail fibers lined up evenly for the tail, take a small bunch between your finger and thumb and slowly pull them away from the shaft of the feather until all the points are level. Then still holding the bunch tight so the points remain level, cut them away from the feather shaft with one swift cut.

4 Tie in the tail fibers on top of the hook shank. Three turns of tying thread over the tail and two under.
The tail should be approximately two-thirds of the hook shank length.

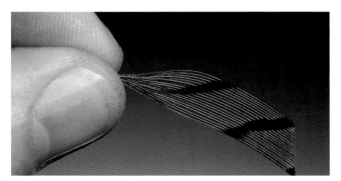

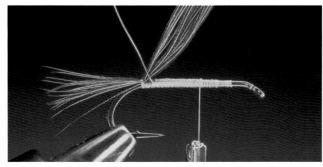

5 Cut a 10cm length of fine copper wire. Tie in the copper wire along the whole length of the hook shank, finishing just before the tail base.

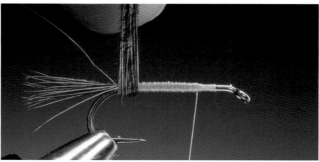

6 Before you start to wind over the abdomen, take your copper wire and swing it under and onto the back side of the hook, as shown. Before you begin wrapping the pheasant tail fibers to form the abdomen, make sure that all the fibers are parallel, and not twisted or crossing over each other!

7 Once you have wrapped the fibers two-thirds the length of the hook shank, tie them off as shown with four or five tight turns of tying thread over the fibers and two in front of the fibers on the hook shank. This will lock the tying thread and stop it from slipping.

8 Take hold of the copper wire and make one turn in the opposite direction you wound the pheasant tail fibers, around the tail base—then four or five open turns to form the rib. When you come to the remaining tuft of fibers at the thorax, make several tight turns of wire along the remaining hook shank, stopping about 3mm from the hook eye.

9 Trim off the tuft of fibers and cover the bare copper wire with a few wraps of tying thread.

10 Now cut another slightly larger bunch of tail fibers and tie them in a little way into the abdomen on top of the hook shank.

11 Cut two or three peacock herls from just under the eye of the peacock tail feather. The herl found here is much stronger than it is lower down the tail feather.

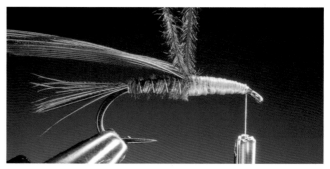

12 Trim off the excess fibers from the wing case. Tie in the peacock herls, butt ends first, and cover the ends with tying thread towards the hook eye.

Continued page 44

13 Take the peacock herl and wrap them over the whole thorax making sure they don't twist and cross each other. Tie off behind the hook eye and cut off the excess.

14 Cut a small bunch of pheasant tail fibers and tie in as shown, just behind the hook eye on the side of the thorax.

15 Trim off the excess fiber and repeat step 14 on the other side of the thorax.

16 Now take the bunch of pheasant tail fibers you tied in for the wing case, and fold them over the thorax. Again take care to make sure that all the fibers are parallel and don't cross over each other. Secure with a few turns of tying thread.

17 Trim off the fibers over the hook eye, about the same length as the hook eye and whip finish. Remove the tying thread and coat the whippings with a small drop of varnish.

18 The finished pheasant tail nymph as seen from above. Note the proportions and symmetry in the tail, body, wing case, and legs.

3

Burrowing Mayfly Nymph

Ostrich herl gills • Yarn wing casing • CDC legs

Although many nymph patterns today are intended to imitate a wide spectrum of aquatic foods rather than the nymphal stage of just one specific species, this pattern imitates the final nymphal stage of the largest burrowing mayflies *Ephemera guttulata* (Green Drake) and *Ephemera simulans* (Brown Drake) and the European relatives *Ephemera danica* and *vulgata*.

These nymphs prefer soft organic or sandy and muddy bottoms, where they can live buried for several years, only appearing occasionally to feed on decomposing vegetable and plant matter. They have been known to burrow as deep as 15 meters.

These large nymphs which range from 12 to 32mm in length, can be recognised easily by the breathing gills along the sides of their lower body, and by their oversized fore legs which are adapted for burrowing.

The gills however are not only used for breathing but also function as a ventilation system for the tunnel the nymphs dig, keeping water flowing through it, which in turn keeps it open. If the nymph leaves its burrow or stops the undulating movement of the gills, the burrow collapses shortly afterwards.

These nymphs are inaccessible to the trout for most of their lifecycle, but one of these on your leader at the correct time can make the difference between great sport and no sport.

When the time comes for them to leave the safety of their burrows, swimming quickly with an undulating body movement (something ostrich herl and CDC imitate beautifully) towards the surface, trout can feed on this ascending nymphal stage for several hours before turning onto the sub-imago winged stage.

The weight placed under the thorax of the nymph helps emulate their undulating swimming action when pulled through the water with short pauses.

When it comes to tying these large nymphs, your hook choice should reflect the natural body length, so a 3XL or a 4XL hook in a size 8-12 works well.

The dubbing used for the rear body and the thorax should be one that absorbs water, rather than a water-repellent dry fly dubbing.

A trick that helps to get the nymph down, after you have tied it on your leader, is to give it a few seconds in the water and then squeeze it hard between your finger and thumb to press out any trapped air that may be caught in the dubbing and CDC.

I also like to use a UV-treated dubbing and ostrich herl. It does no harm in giving the pattern that extra edge that may make a difference.

Previously I have used golden pheasant center tail fibers for the wing case but these have proved to be a little too fragile for the small sharp teeth of trout, so I have substituted it with Antron body wool.

Antron is a type of nylon that has a trilobal cross-section so that each single fiber is three-sided, rather like the three-pointed star in the Mercedes emblem.

When many Antron fibers are woven together into a yarn, the multiple tiny facets of every strand reflect light in all directions, enhancing color. Available in more colors than imaginable, and inexpensive, this

TECHNIQUES MASTERED

- **Ostrich herl gills**
  Ribbing the abdomen with a long bushy-fibered ostrich herl to create ultra-realistic, pulsating nymph body gills.

- **Antron wing case**
  Creating a large wing case of Antron yarn that mimicks the correct profile: broad at the abdomen and slim at the head.

- **CDC thorax and legs**
  How to spin a large tapered CDC dubbing brush using a Magic Tool to form the nymph's thorax and legs.

makes it an ideal flytying material with a multitude of applications.

Using natural colors for wing cases on nymphs or dry flies, a few fibers can be tied in as a trailing shuck on nymphs and emergers.

The trilobal fibers trap small pockets of air, creating a very realistic gas bubble effect. In the more vivid fluorescent colors this Antron can be used as hot spots and tags. It can be twisted and wrapped to form life-like segmented caddis pupae bodies and even melted to form the heads of a peeping caddis.

Tying the Burrowing Mayfly Nymph

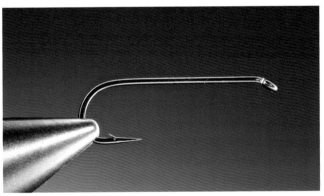

1 Secure your 3XL or 4XL nymph hook in the vise, making sure that it is horizontal.

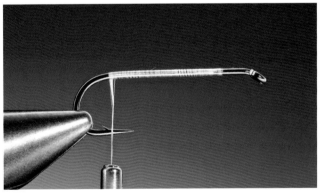

2 Attach your tying thread and cover the whole shank until the thread is hanging between the hook barb and point.

3 Take some small, medium or large-size lead wire, depending on your hook size and weighting requirements.

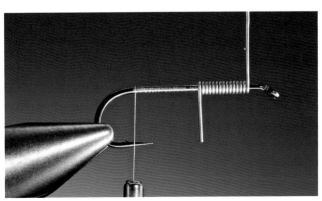

4 Wind on a short length of lead wire under the thorax, covering approximately a third of the hook shank.

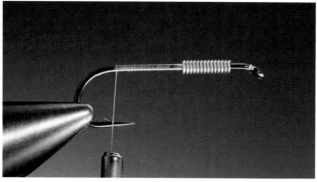

5 Once the lead wire is wound and packed tight, trim off the surplus.

6 For the tails of the nymph you will need some olive ostrich herl. Here I like to use a UV-treated herl to give the nymph an extra edge.

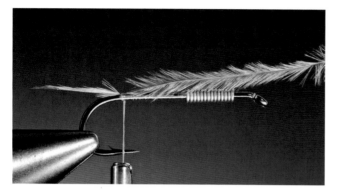

7 Select three herls with even tips. Tie in the first herl on top center of the hook shank. Again, this should be about a third of the length of the hook shank.

8 Now tie in the other two herls, one on each side of the center tail.

9 Tie down the remaining herl along the whole hook shank and cut away the excess herl.

10 Select another long herl with nice long fibers for the ribbing, which will represent the nymph's gills.

11 Now spin some Antron dubbing tightly onto the tying thread. Make sure that this is tight so that the finished body is dense.

12 Continue with the Antron dubbing and build up a tapered rear body along two-thirds of the hook shank.

13 Wind on the ostrich herl as a rib over the rear body part, making sure that the herl fibers stand out at 90 degrees from the hook shank. Make about six to seven tight, even turns, then tie off at the thorax.

14 Remove the excess herl and carefully trim off the herl fibers on the top of the body only, as shown. This is not necessary but gives a little more realistic look to the nymph.

15 The trimmed rear body should now look like this from the side.

16 And like this from above, with the gills prominent along each side of the body.

17 Now cut four lengths of floss or Antron body wool and tie these in as shown along the top of the thorax. These will form the wing case later.

18 Trim off the ends of the floss behind the hook eye and tie down. Wind the tying thread back towards the rear body.

19 Dub the whole thorax quite heavily and return the tying thread once again to the junction between the thorax and the rear body. Take care that you leave about 2 to 3mm space behind the hook eye to tie off the wing case later.

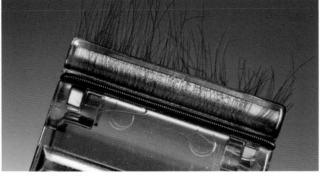

20 Place a large CDC hackle in a Magic Tool Clip. Notice how the CDC fibers taper in length from long on the left side, getting shorter to the right.

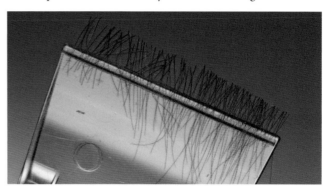

21 Transfer the CDC to the second Magic Tool Clip ready for use.

22 Now spin the CDC with the longest fibers at the top of the dubbing loop. These are to be wound in the thorax first for the longest legs.

23 Wind on the CDC dubbing brush in open, even turns through the thorax to form the legs.

24 Taking hold of all four pieces of floss, fold them over the thorax and secure with a couple of turns of tying thread. Pull once again to tighten up the wing case and secure with a few more turns of tying thread.

25 Trim off the excess floss and tie down the ends. If you are using Dyneema or another GSP thread, you can color it black with a permanent felt marker.

26 Whip finish and remove the tying thread. Finish off with a drop of varnish. This is the finished olive mayfly nymph.

27 The finished red mayfly nymph.

28 The finished grey mayfly nymph.

4

Klinkhamer

Parachute hackling • Post tips • Making the vise work for you

It was in Norway on June 27, 1984, that the first Klinkhamer Special was born, from the vise of my old friend Hans van Klinken. He designed it for fishing grayling in the river Glomma. It is now regarded as a modern classic and a standard pattern for all trout and grayling fishing the world over, and is probably the best and most adaptable emerger to date. The parachute style is said to instill a sense of urgency and induce a take in a feeding fish before their snack takes flight.

Can you show me how to tie a Klinkhamer? is up in the top five requests from people when I am doing tying demos, along with: *What's the correct way to tie a parachute hackle without a gallows tool?* I normally tie the Klinkhamer to demonstrate both.

Preparation and material choice are important if you are to achieve the correct body shape and hackle, both of which determine the desired emerger presentation of the fly when fished.

Firstly, the correct hook should be used, one with a curved shank, wide gape, slightly heavy wire and a straight eye. Hans has his own Klinkhamer hooks specially designed for this pattern: Daiichi 1160.

The posts on parachute patterns have several functions: first and foremost as a foundation around which the horizontal hackle can be wound; but also as an upright wing on both dry flies and emergers. This post, in combination with the slightly heavy wire hook, keeps the pattern on an even keel when fished. It's also a great sight indicator which helps you to follow the fly at a distance, in low light conditions and in rough water.

The rear of the post, if trimmed correctly, will also be the foundation for our slender tapered dubbed body. When wrapping the base of the post, in preparation to accommodate the hackle, this needs to be nice and firm. A drop of varnish or head cement will help with this.

A problem with the "traditional parachute hackle" is finishing it neatly. You usually have to wind your tying thread forward through the thorax and hold the hackle fibers out of the way when you whip finish. This method avoids all that and results in a para perfect hackle.

Your saddle hackle should be prepared by stripping off 10mm of the fibers from one side and 60-70mm of the fibers from the other (step 11). This will ensure that when wrapped, the hackle fibers will have maximum surface contact when fished, keeping the body and thorax of the fly just under the water where they belong.

Before you begin wrapping the hackle, re-position your hook in the vise from its original horizontal position to vertical. This makes wrapping a parachute hackle as easy as wrapping a traditional collar hackle! Re-attach your tying thread at the base of the post, and wind it down, close into the thorax. If you have a material clip on your vise, once your thread is secure, hang it out of the way (step 19).

 Now wrap your hackle as you would a traditional dry fly collar hackle, taking care that each turn of hackle is close to the previous one, all the way down into the thorax.

When you reach the thorax, release your tying thread from the material clip and make one wrap over the hackle and one wrap under to secure it. Trim away the surplus hackle.

Now trim your post to the required length, take your whip finish tool and make one whip finish, between the hackle and the thorax, taking care not to trap any hackle fibers.

Before you make the second and last whip finish, place a small drop of varnish on the tying thread closed to the thorax. This varnish will be drawn into the whip finish as you tighten, and secure it. The result should be a perfect parachute hackle.

TECHNIQUES MASTERED

- **Para-post skills**
  Learn the correct setting of the post and how to use the rear of the surplus para-post to form a perfect tapered underbody as a foundation for the dubbed overbody.

- **Perfecting the para hackle**
  Easy and trouble-free method of mounting and wrapping a parachute hackle without the use of a gallows tool.

- **Vertical whip finishing**
  Whip finishing a parachute hackle with the hook vertical in the vise, a method which avoids trapping hackle barbs.

Two of the best post materials are Para-post and Aero Dry Wing which are available in many colors.

Tying the Klinkhamer

THE DRESSING

Hook: Mustad C49S #6-14
Thread: Olive
Post: Para-post or Aero dry wing
Body: Olive super-fine dubbing
Thorax: Peacock herl
Hackle: Whiting silver badger saddle

WATCH THE VIDEO

youtu.be/sTKCB6R3T_c

Tying the Klinkhamer with
Barry Ord Clarke

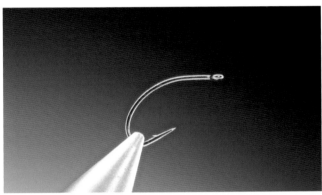

1 Secure your dry fly hook in the vise, as shown, with the hook shank horizontal.

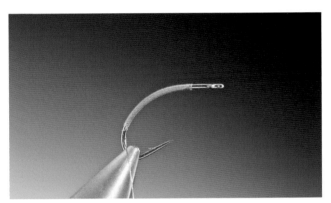

2 Run a fine foundation of tying thread along the hook shank.

3 Return your tying thread back up to the thorax position.

4 Select your chosen post material and color. The Aero dry wing material is extremely expensive but the Veniard alternative is just as good and a third of the price.

5 Cut a few strands of your post material, four for a #8 hook.

6 Tie these in as shown at the correct position for the post.

7 Make sure that you have enough post material at the rear of the post to hold.

8 While holding the rear post material in one hand, trim off the ends at a slight angle, so when covered with tying thread they will make a tapered body.

9 Even up the body with tying thread to a slight taper. Make a few turns with tying thread tight into the front of the post, so it rises 90 degrees from the hook shank.

10 Spin some dubbing onto your tying thread and make a neat tapered body which finishes just before the thorax.

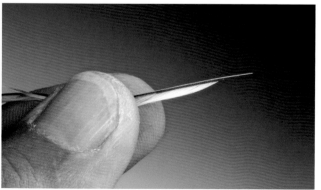

11 Select and prepare a hackle. When tying large Klinkhamers, I like to use a slightly over-sized hackle.

12 Now using your tying thread, strengthen the post's base by first wrapping up and then down again.

KILNKHAMER

13 If you would like to give the post an even better foundation to wind on your hackle, place a tiny drop of varnish onto the wrappings.

14 Now tie in the hackle at the base of the post.

15 Wrap your tying thread back to the rear of the thorax and tie in a few strands of peacock herl. Return your tying thread to just behind the hook eye.

16 Wrap the peacock herl forward to form the thorax. Tie off just behind the hook eye.

17 Trim away any remaining herl, whip finish and remove your tying thread.

18 Remove the hook from the vise and replace as shown. Now re-attach your tying thread to the post's base and wind down close to the thorax.

19 Hang your tying thread to one side and start wrapping your hackle down the post base.

20 Make sure that you wrap your hackle with each turn under but tight into the last turn, all the way down to the thorax.

21 Tie off the hackle between the thorax and the last turn of hackle. Remove the surplus hackle, and trim down the post to the desired length.

22 Using a whip finish tool, make a whip finish or two just below the hackle. Take care not to trap any of the hackle barbules. Just before you tighten your whip finish knot, place a drop of varnish on your tying thread close to the thorax and then tighten.

23 Remove your tying thread.

24 Klinkhamer from below.

25 Klinkhamer from above.

Klinkhopper

This is my adaptation of the Klinkhamer pattern for a grasshopper imitation.

VARIANT

THE DRESSING

Hook: Mustad C49 6-14
Thread: Dark green
Post: Para-post
Body: Bright green dubbing
Rib: Tying thread dubbing loop
Wing: Yellow dyed partridge hackle
Legs: Yellow pheasant tail fibres
Thorax: Olive ostrich herl
Hackle: Yellow dyed grizzly hackle

WATCH THE VIDEO

youtu.be/FkJmbiXUGDk

Tying the Klinkhopper with
Barry Ord Clarke

AND HOPPER LEGS VIDEO

youtu.be/EDZ6xZ6ogoQ

Tying Knots in Daddy Legs
with Barry Ord Clarke

1 Tie the post and body as for the Klinkhamer, but leave a dubbing loop of tying thread at the tail of the hook as shown.

2 Wind the tying thread rib in evenly-spaced turns and tie off at the thorax.

3 Make a set of two hopper legs with yellow dyed pheasant tail.

4 Take a nicely marked yellow dyed partridge hackle and coat with UV resin.

5 Cut a small V out of the end of the hackle to make the hopper wing.

6 Firstly tie in the wing and then one leg each side.

7 Tie in the hackle at post base and the ostrich herl at the rear of the thorax.

8 Wrap the ostrich herl forward to form the thorax and tie off behind the hook eye. Whip finish and remove your tying thread.

9 Follow steps 18 to 23 for Klinkhamer.

10 The finished Klinkhopper.

5

CDC and Deer Hair Emerger

Turkey biot bodies • CDC and deer hair winging

An emerger is, you could say, the final act of most aquatic pupae and nymphs, in their transition from life in an aquatic environment to one on dry land.

When mayfly nymphs are ready to hatch they accumulate a buoyant gas under their exoskeleton. This not only separates the exoskeleton from the encased insect's emerging body but, as this gas increases, it helps the nymph become more buoyant and start its ascent, which the nymph assists with a rapid, undulating swimming action towards the surface. Breaching the film can take from just a few seconds to fifteen minutes.

At this stage, many emergers fail to make it. Hence the intensity and huge numbers in hatches. Whether for seconds or minutes, the whole time the struggling insect is stuck in the film, it's drifting downstream over feeding fish.

It is here that it is at its most vulnerable.

When it comes to tying emergers, it's extremely important that whatever pattern you use to imitate the final stages of a hatching mayfly, it gives a legitimate footprint and floats in the correct manner. All this is achieved with this pattern. The body should hang in the top water column, as with a Klinkhamer. The spiky hare's ear dubbing on the thorax is an excellent guise for legs. The wing should stay above the surface. This not only gives the impression of the emerging upright wings from the exoskeleton, which some say induces a sense of "urgency" in a feeding trout, but it also acts as a sight indicator for the angler.

If you follow these pointers and make a good choice of materials, you will have greater success with your own emerger patterns.

It's the wing on this pattern that will keep everything on an even keel and which enables correct presentation. I like to use a deer hair that is a little stiffer and shorter than normal with nicely marked barred tips. These are found in abundance on a deer mask, but similar hair is also marketed as Comparadun deer hair. This hair doesn't flare as much as spinning hair when placed under pressure from the tying thread and makes for a neat, compact, stiff wing.

The CDC rear wing is added for that little extra buoyancy. Here I also like to use natural CDC that hasn't been washed, dyed or processed in any other way. These retain the optimal amount of the duck's preening oil and float substantially better.

The sub-surface tail and abdomen also have a role to play. The speckled partridge tail should be sparse. These beautifully marked fibers create a splendid illusion of tails, in both color and movement.

For the larger mayflies, the turkey biots are highly recommended for their longer length of quill. But if you intend to tie on smaller hook sizes, then smaller, and easily obtainable goose biots can be used.

Biots can be found on all birds. They are the short stiff barbs located on the leading edge of the outer vane of all primary wing feathers. Only two species provide those that are most commonly used by the fly tyer. These are the turkey and the goose.

Goose biots are normally too short for wrapping a decent quill body, but are put to significant use as tails and antenna on various nymphs and wing buds on buzzers and midge larvae.

Turkey biots are considerably larger than goose biots, and make easy work when it comes to wrapping bodies. Once you have chosen a biot, you

- **Partridge hackle barb tail**
  How to select and prepare a speckled brown partridge hackle to make a small mayfly emerger tail.

- **Turkey biot segmented body**
  Correct method for mounting and wrapping a turkey biot to form a large quill mayfly emerger body.

- **CDC and deer hair wing**
  Selection and preparation of deer hair for making a raised mixed deer hair and CDC emerger wing.

will notice that one side has a slightly sloping edge.

There are two ways to tie in your biot. For a smooth body, this angled edge has to be wrapped against the hook shank. For a ribbed, segmented body as with this pattern, the angled edge is wrapped away from the hook shank.

Tying the CDC and Deer Hair Emerger

....
THE DRESSING
....

Hook: Mustad C49S #10-16
Thread: Olive
Wing: Natural deer hair & CDC
Tail: Speckled partridge
Body: Olive turkey biot
Thorax: Hare's ear and Antron dubbing mix

....
WATCH THE VIDEO
....

youtu.be/3ABafzWjFDU
Tying the CDC & Deer Hair
Emerger with Barry Ord Clarke

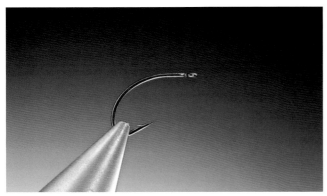

1 Secure your curved emerger hook in the vise, as shown, with the hook shank horizontal.

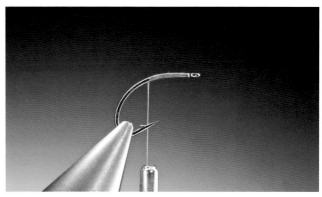

2 Run a fine foundation of tying thread along the front half of the hook shank.

3 Cut a small bunch of fine stiff deer hair and even up the tips in a hair stacker. I find the wing looks better if you have deer hair with barred tips.

4 Tie the small bunch of deer hair in on top of the hook shank a little distance back from the hook eye. Trim off the butt ends at a slight angle.

5 Cover the butt ends of the deer hair with tying thread to form a smooth tapered underbody.

6 Select 1 to 3 CDC hackles, depending on the hook size and lay them flat on top of each other with the tips level.

7 Tie the CDC hackles in just behind the deer hair as shown. Secure them with a couple of loose turns of tying thread and then pull them back carefully, so they are just a little longer or the same length as the deer hair wing.

8 Trim away the surplus CDC, again at an angle, and wrap the tying thread back down the hook bend.

9 Now select a well-marked speckled partridge feather for the tail. Prepare by cutting away the tip as shown.

10 Strip a small bunch of fibers from the partridge hackle and tie in to make a short tail. Build up a smooth tapered underbody with tying thread.

11 These stripped wild turkey biots from Nature's Spirit are some of the best I have ever seen.

12 Tie the biot in by the tip, at the tail base. If you would like to make the body a little more robust, give the underbody a fine coat with varnish or superglue glue, before you wrap the quill.

Continued page 68

13 Attach a hackle plier and wrap the quill in even, neat, touching turns all the way up to the thorax. Tie off.

14 Apply a little dubbing to your tying thread and start wrapping the thorax forward, towards the wing.

15 Make sure that you cover behind, under and forward of the wing with dubbing.

16 Make a few wraps of tying thread to form a little neat head and whip finish. Snip off your tying thread.

17 The emerger viewed from above. Here you can see the correct proportions. Slender tail, segmented and tapered body, spiky thorax, and a symmetrical fan-shaped wing.

6

Vulgata Emerger

Moose mane bodies • XL parachute hackling • Para post perfecting

Emergers are one the most attractive stages of a mayfly lifecycle for feeding trout and grayling. This stage is very precarious for the insect, when many things can go wrong and leave the hatching mayfly stuck in the surface film struggling to break free from its larval shuck–making them easy pickings for predatory fish.

This stage can often be recognised during a hatch by steadily rising trout, sipping in emergers from just under the surface.

This is a pattern I use for most of the larger mayflies such as *vulgata* and *danica*. Like the Klinkhamer, it functions as both emerger and attractor.

Even though these emergers are the first choice for feeding fish, it's still crucial that you have a realistic pattern that won't be rejected by selective trout. As you may have noticed by now, I am a great fan of moose mane bodies, especially when it comes to imitating mayflies. With the correct choice of color of moose mane hair, you are able to imitate just about any mayfly body beautifully and very realistically.

Just a few of the combinations I use can be seen on page 85.

This emerger I prefer to tie Klinkhamer-style, for obvious presentational reasons: the parachute hackle supporting the abdomen and thorax that are presented hanging in the surface.

To the pattern shown here, you can also add a trailing shuck if you wish, just a few strands of polypropylene yarn, only a few mm long, tied in as a tail at the rear of the abdomen. This is meant to imitate the shuck that the insect is trying to cast, and break free from.

When buying a patch of natural moose mane, look for a good overall length of hair. Longer hair is much easier to handle when tying and will of course make larger quill-style bodies.

Look also for a wonderful salt and pepper mix of white, grey, brown and jet black hairs. Tying two or more hairs in, one dark and one or two light in color by the tips and wrapping them as one, creates great segmented bodies. Nature's Spirit have a large selection of excellent natural and natural white dyed moose mane patches, in all the important mayfly colors.

TECHNIQUES MASTERED

- **Moose mane segmented body**
  Wrapping a simple but effective moose mane hair segmented mayfly body.

- **Para post perfecting**
  Getting the correct setting of the post and using the rear of the surplus para post to form a perfect tapered underbody as a foundation for the moose mane hair overbody.

- **XL Parachute hackle**
  Mounting and using a extra-large parachute hackle for better presentation and buoyancy of an emerger.

Tying the Vulgata Emerger

....
THE DRESSING
....

Hook: Mustad C49S #8-12
Thread: Dyneema
Body: Three moose mane hairs
Post: Para post yarn
Thorax: Peacock herl
Hackle: Silver badger

....
WATCH THE VIDEO
....

youtu.be/PBOyga1Kzgg
Tying the Vulgata Emerger with
Barry Ord Clarke

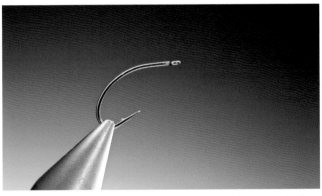

1 Secure your emerger hook in the vise, as shown, with the hook shank horizontal.

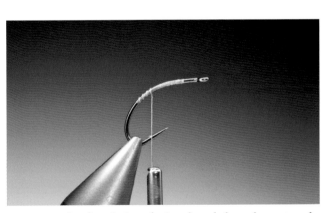

2 Run a fine foundation of tying thread along the center of the hook shank.

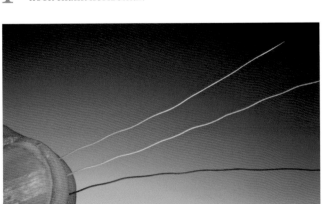

3 Select three long moose mane hairs, two light and one black. Align the moose mane hair tips, then trim the butt ends, so all three hairs are the same length.

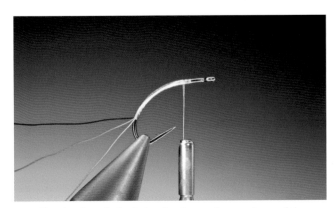

4 Tie the three hairs in by the tips at the very base of the hook bend. Make sure that all three hair tips are close to each other. Wrap your tying thread forward to just behind the hook eye.

5 Cut a length of para post yarn, approximately 5-6cm long. Depending on which post yarn you use, you may have to double it, to make the post more dense. Tie this in about 5mm behind the hook eye.

6 Once secure, trim the rear of the para post yarn at an angle. Doing this will give the abdomen an increasing taper towards the thorax.

7 Spin your bobbin holder anti-clockwise, so your tying thread gets a flat profile. Now cover the hook shank with tying thread, giving underbody a smooth finish and taper.

8 Wrap your tying thread forward and make a few wraps close in front of the para wing post. This will support the para post 90 degrees to the hook shank.

9 Holding all three hairs at once, carefully wrap them in tight neat turns up over the body. Take care not to twist or cross the hairs over each other.

10 Once the whole body is complete, tie off the hairs at the thorax. You should have a nice segmented body effect.

11 Trim away the excess moose mane hairs. Using tying thread, wrap the base of the para post about 4 or 5mm up the yarn. Return the tying thread to the rear of the thorax. You can strengthen the post base by coating it with a drop of varnish.

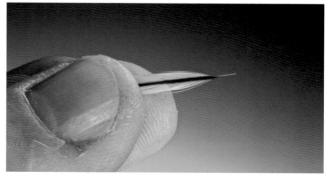

12 Select and prepare a silver badger saddle hackle as shown. I like to use one that is a little larger than normal for the hook size.

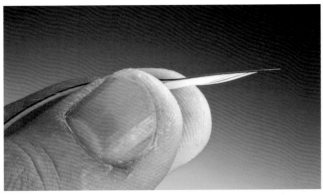

13 Now strip off approximately 50mm of the fibers from one side of the hackle.

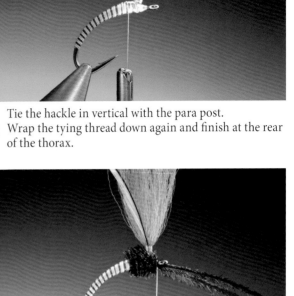

14 Tie the hackle in vertical with the para post. Wrap the tying thread down again and finish at the rear of the thorax.

15 Tie in two long peacock herls a little into the moose hair abdomen. Wrap your tying thread forward, right behind the hook eye.

16 Attach a hackle plier to both the peacock herls and carefully wrap in tight neat turns forward, taking care not to twist them. Tie off right behind the hook eye.

17 Trim away the excess herl, whip finish and remove your tying thread.

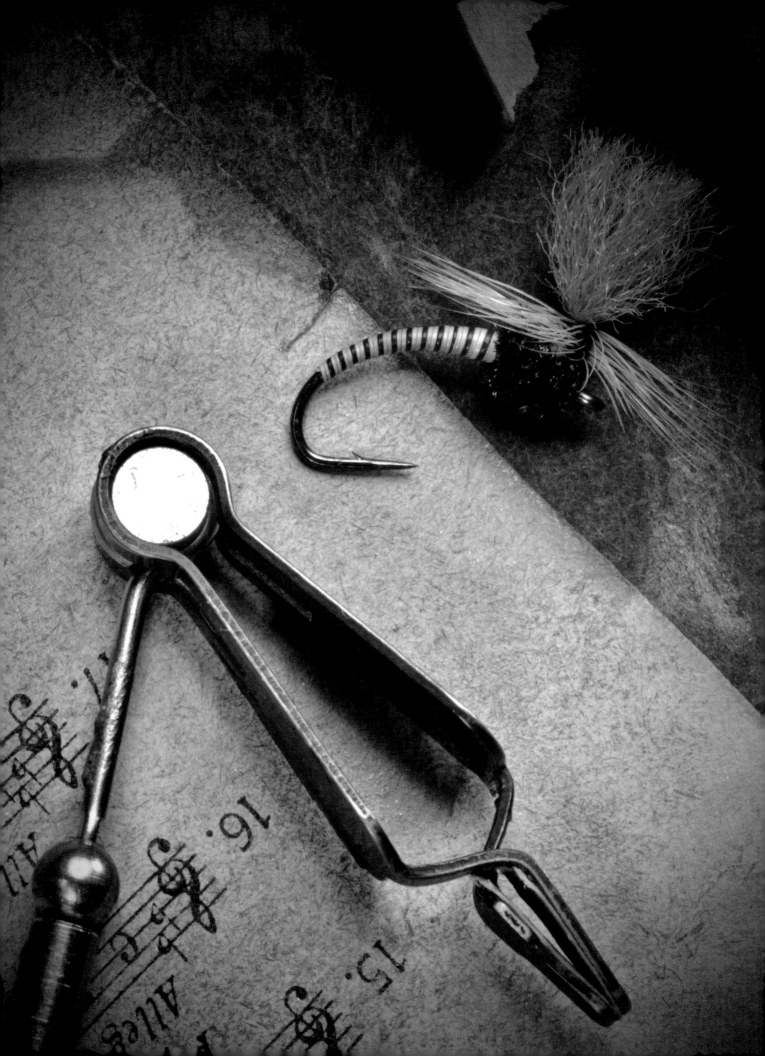

18 Rotate the hook in your vise and re-attach your tying thread to the para post base and wind down, close in to the thorax.

19 Using a hackle plier, carefully wrap your hackle down the para post base. Take care that each turn of hackle is close into the previous turn with as little space between each turn as possible. Tie off the hackle at the thorax.

20 Cut away excess hackle and trim the para post to the desired length. Make a whip finish, between the hackle and the thorax, taking care not to trap any hackle fibers. Place a drop of varnish on your tying thread close to the thorax and make one last whip finish.

21 Rotate the hook in the vise again and snip off your tying thread.

22 View from below showing the exaggerated hackle.

Wally Wing Dun

Moose mane "quills" • Wally Wing construction • Reverse collar hackling

Movements and trends come and go, and the fashion and design industry are not alone when it comes to reviving past styles. We fly tyers are constantly rediscovering, reinventing and repopularizing patterns from the past. I believe the use of social media within the flytying world has accelerated this.

When I began tying flies I had two or three 'go-to' books which contained just about all the patterns I tied. Now, with the likes of internet, Facebook, and YouTube, to name just a few, we have access to detailed tying instruction for just about every pattern ever known, and then some. Combine this with contemporary materials, modern hook styles, new techniques and the collective creativity of the fly tyers of the world, and good things are bound to happen!

In this chapter I illustrate one of those techniques that has recently become extremely popular again,

after being more or less shelved for over four decades.

The original Wally Wing was created by Canadian tyer Wally Lutz in the early 1970s. This winging technique falls under the category of "reverse hackle wings" along with Wonder Wings and Origami Wings.

Although all three styles have similar characteristics, the latter two require two hackles for a pair of wings, and just about any type of hackle or feather with long enough barbs can be used for this technique, whereas both wings are made for the Wally Wing with a single feather.

We are also restricted here as to which feathers can be used for the Wally Wing splitting technique. The easiest to use are the flank feathers from various waterfowl.

Your choice of winging material for tying Wally Wings is paramount, if you wish to succeed!

If you have purchased a packet with mixed mallard or teal flank, only a limited number of these will be usable. I recommend purchasing a packet of select flank or a whole mallard drake skin. Having a whole skin has many advantages. The price of a whole skin is nominal when you think of what you pay for a little packet "stuffed" with feathers that only weigh a couple of grams. All the feathers are perfectly packaged by nature on a skin, keeping them all in the same direction and neatly stacked on top of each other. This also makes selection of individual feathers in the size required easier.

If you feel the investment of a whole skin is beyond your budget, consider purchasing one as a collective with other flytying friends and splitting it.

There is a mixed school of thought in the flytying and fishing fraternity when it comes to fishing with Wally Wing patterns. Some say they are hopeless and constantly twist the leader under casting; others, like my good friend and world-class fly tyer Trevor Jones, who has been one of the pioneers behind the renaissance of this pattern, swear by them. No matter what your opinion may be, I think we can all agree that they make a beautiful fly and are fun to tie.

Regarding the technique I have developed here to tie Wally Wings, you need a small plastic tube to hold

TECHNIQUES MASTERED

- **Match the hatch bodies**
  Choosing, using and mixing moose mane hairs to make realistic colored mayfly bodies with delicate color gradation and segmenting.

- **Wally Wings**
  How to prepare, and with the help of a simple technique, mount and split mallard flank feathers to make perfect Wally Wings.

- **Reverse collar hackle**
  Choice, preparation and setting of a reverse-wound thorax hackle.

the barbs in place for tying in. I have experimented with several types of tube for executing this technique and have found the absolute best is a tapered reserve nozzle from a small bottle of UV resin.

Depending on what size of Wally Wings you intend to tie, you first have to adjust the tip opening of the nozzle to the correct size of feather to be used. This is simply achieved by preparing a flank feather, as in step 15, then seeing if you can pass it all the way through the tube: you don't want to tie the wings in and not be able to remove the tube because the feather stem is too thick!

Cut a couple of millimeters from the end of the tube and try again. Repeat until the correct nozzle opening is attained.

OOOMDGFS-258-D
MALLARD DUCK
SELECTED SMALL
GREY FLANK
NATURAL

Tying the Wally Wing Dun

THE DRESSING

Hook: Mustad C53S #10-14
Thread: Grey
Tail: Coq de Leon
Wings: Mallard flank
Body: One black and two brown
  moose mane hairs
Thorax: Peacock herl
Hackle: Whiting Silver badger saddle

WATCH THE VIDEO

youtu.be/8xu0tiyoWnI
Tying the Wally Wing Dun
with Barry Ord Clarke

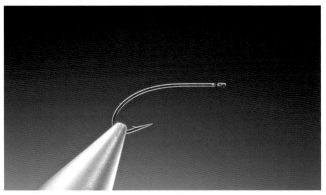

1 Secure your dry fly hook in the vise, as shown, with the hook shank horizontal.

2 Run a slim foundation of tying thread along the hook shank, as shown.

3 Select a nicely marked Coq de Leon hackle for the tail fibers.

4 Strip a small bunch of Coq de Leon fibers from the hackle to make the tail.

5 Tie in the bunch on top of the hook shank. The tail should be approximately the same length as the hook shank.

6 With a few neat wraps of tying thread, cover the ends of the Coq de Leon.

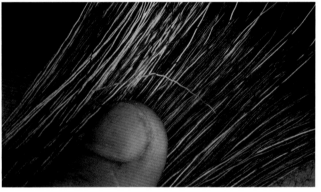

7 When buying a patch of moose mane, look for one that has a nice mixture of natural colors!

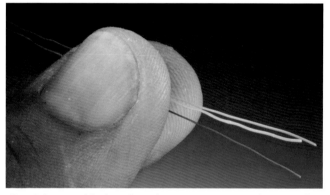

8 Select one black and two brown moose mane hairs. Make sure they are the same length.

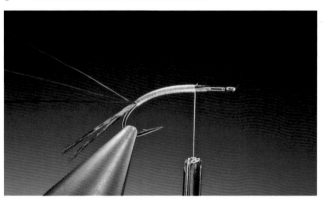

9 Tie these in by the tips, at the tail base, taking care that all three hairs are tied in, touching at the same point.

10 Using neat and even turns of tying thread, build up a slight taper to the underbody.

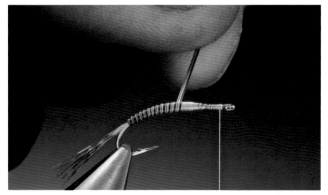

11 Holding all three moose mane hairs together, begin to wrap them up over the hook shank to form the segmented body. Keep the hairs parallel as you wrap, so they don't cross over each other or twist.

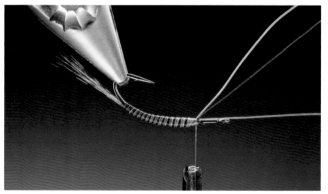

12 Once you have wrapped the whole body, rotate your vise, and tie off the hairs at the thorax with a few firm turns of tying thread.

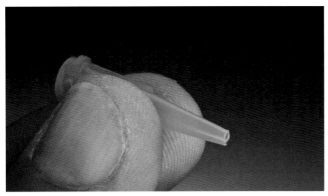

13 Before you start on the wings, you will need a small
plastic tube. This one is from a bottle of UV resin.

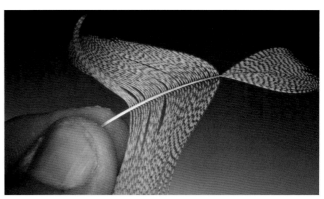

14 Select a mallard flank feather with long barbs and nice
markings. Make sure that there are no short barbs in the
two sections to be used for the wings.

15 Wet the barbs at the tip of the flank feather and pull to
a point.

16 Place the tip into the tube and carefully pull through
until you have the size of wings required.

17 Now keeping the mallard flank in the tube, offer the wings up to the correct position on the thorax and secure with a couple
of turns of tying thread. While retaining tension on your bobbin, carefully position the wings to their final resting place
and secure with a few more turns of thread. Still retaining tension on your bobbin, slide the tube off.

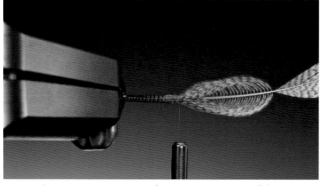

18 Once secure, cut away the remaining stem of the mallard flank feather and tidy up with a few more turns of tying thread.

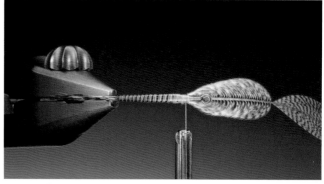

19 This is how the wing should look from the underside of the hook.

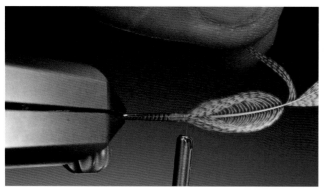

20 Now you are ready to split the wings. Hold the tip of the mallard flank in one hand, then carefully separate the nearest barbs from the tip with the other hand.

21 You should take care here to select only two barbules: no more, no less! Carefully pull the barbs away from the feather stem as shown, until it tears all the way down to the thorax.

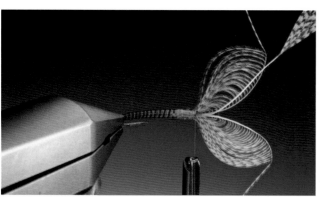

22 Repeat to make the second wing.

23 With a pair of fine-pointed scissors, carefully cut away the center stem and the remaining barbs on the wing tips.

24 Make a few wraps of tying thread tight in front and into the wings, so they lift 90 degrees from the hook shank.

25 Run your tying thread back to the rear of the thorax and tie in a nice bushy peacock herl.

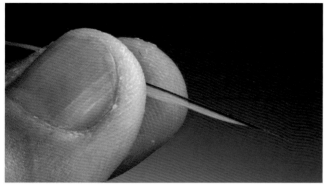

26 Select and prepare a silver badger hackle of the correct size and strip off all the barbs from the side of the hackle that will be wrapped nearest the hook shank.

27 Tie in the hackle slightly forward of the herl so it is possible to get in one or two turns of herl behind the hackle before you go forward and cover the thorax.

28 Without twisting the peacock herl, wind it forward to cover the whole thorax. Tie off and cut away any remaining herl. Secure with a single whip finish.

29 Now wind your hackle through the peacock herl thorax with the barbs pointing forward. This makes the fly sit much better on the water.

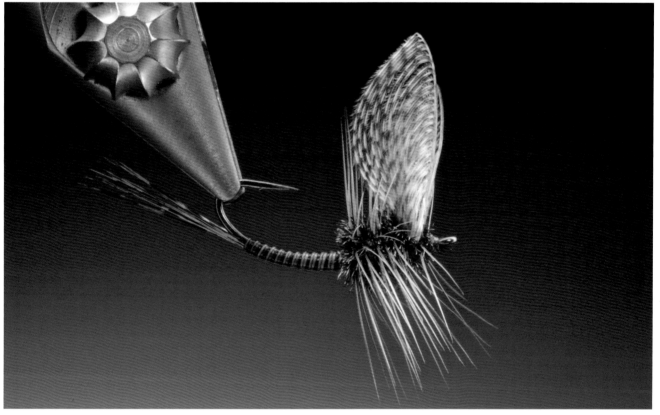

30 Tie off the hackle whip finish and give the head a drop of varnish to finish the fly off.

Customizing mayfly bodies

Here's a simple technique for customizing your mayfly bodies to match the hatch. Just by mixing the correct color combinations of moose mane hairs, you can achieve some very nice body effects.

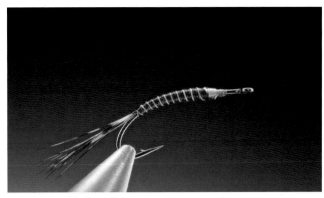

1 Two black and one tan moose mane hairs.

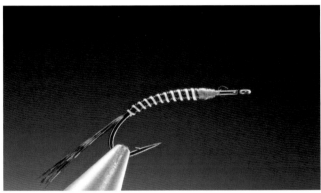

2 Two black and one white moose mane hairs.

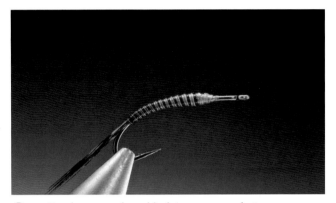

3 Two brown and one black moose mane hairs.

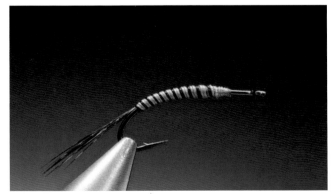

4 Two white and one black moose mane hairs.

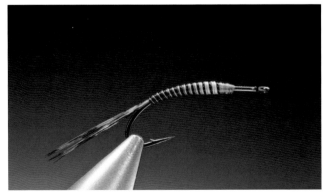

5 For a graded color effect, two brown tipped and one black moose mane hairs.

8

Humpy

Splitting deer hair wings • Mastering the hump • Mixed color hackling

The Humpy and its many popularized variants stem from a pattern called Horner's Deer Hair, for which the tying technique is identical.

This fly is amongst the juiciest of what I like to call "Fatboy" patterns, and finds itself in good company with other chunky flies such as the Royal Wulff and the Streaking Caddis.

Many fly tyers prefer to fish the Humpy rather than tie it, and find the original tying technique, where the overbody (hump) and wings are constructed from the same bunch of deer hair, challenging to master.

So here is a technique I use, not only to simplify the construction, but also to make the pattern a little more durable.

In this variant, I tie in the wings first and I substitute the original deer hair overbody with moose body hair.

One of the advantages of tying the wings in separately is that it makes mastering correct proportions of the fly easier. Although deer hair is one of the most versatile natural materials when used in this way to form the overbody, it is extremely vulnerable to damage by the small sharp teeth of trout.

Moose body hair, on the other hand, although not quite as buoyant as deer hair, still floats well and is far more durable. A good number of flytying books will also recommend that you give the "hump" a coat or two with varnish or head cement, but I personally think this does nothing for the fly's durability, buoyancy—or aesthetics for that matter.

When buying moose body hair, look for a patch of straight hair that has a good, dense, springy feel to it, a solid color, a nice glossy sheen and fine tapered straight tips. This is not only useful for tailing a huge amount of dry fly patterns but perfect for the overbody of the Humpy.

For split deer hair dry fly wings I prefer to use a stiffer, shorter Comparadun-type hair. This won't flare as much as regular deer hair, but will stand erect, giving the appropriate wing profile desired. I also like this hair to have nicely marked tips.

This is not easy to see when on the hide, but pulling a small bunch 90 degrees from the hide so the tips are somewhat even, will give you a good indication, before purchasing. When a small bunch is cleaned and the tips are evened up in a hair stacker, the attractive barred tips stand out and give the wing another dimension. Comparadun hair is normally too short for the original Humpy overbody technique, but is perfect for split up-winged flies.

When it comes to the hackle, this pattern is also listed as "Adams Humpy" because of the mixed brown and grizzly hackles. For this I prefer to use Whiting dry fly saddle, especially for these "Fatboy" patterns when a larger hackle length and sweet spot is an advantage and a big, bushy, dense hackle is desired.

Instead of using two hackles, one brown and one grizzly, you can also use what is known as an "instant Adams" hackle, as I do in the accompanying video. This can be a Grizzly brown variant or a dark Cree hackle: both these hackle types can contain all the colors needed for an Adams in a single hackle.

Tying the Humpy

THE DRESSING

Hook: Mustad R30 #10-16
Thread: Yellow or chosen body color
Wing: Fine stiff natural deer hair
Tail: Moose body hair
Underbody: Bright yellow floss
Overbody: Moose body hair
Hackle: Brown and grizzly mixed

WATCH THE VIDEO

youtu.be/hcldoK0dJMU

Tying the Humpy by Barry Ord Clarke

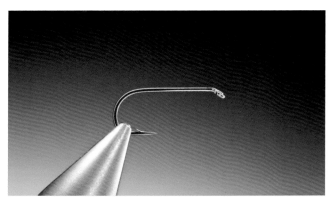

1   Secure your dry fly hook in the vise, as shown, with the hook shank horizontal.

2   Run a fine foundation of tying thread along the front third of the hook shank.

3   Select and clean a bunch of deer hair for the wing. Take care to remove all the underfur and short hairs.

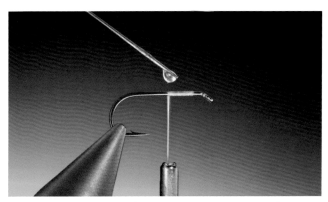

4   Place a small drop of varnish or head cement on the foundation of tying thread. This will help secure the wing and stop the hair slipping.

5 Once clean, stack the deer hair in a small hair stacker, so the tips are all level. Measure the wing.

6 Tie in the bunch of deer hair on top of the hook shank as shown. Secure with a few turns of tying thread.

7 Once secure, trim away the butt ends of the deer hair at a slight taper.

8 Place another drop of varnish on the trimmed butt ends of the deer hair. This will secure the wings and extend the life of the fly.

9 Even up the butt ends of the deer hair with tying thread to a slight taper. Make a few turns with tying thread tight into the front of the wing, so it rises 90 degrees from the hook shank.

10 Separate the deer hair into two even amounts to form the wings. Separate and secure the wings with a figure of eight criss-crossing of tying thread, encircling the base of each, thus forming two divided wings. View from above the wings.

11 Place another small drop of varnish inbetween the wings.

12 Select a small bunch of straight stiff moose body hairs, approximately ten.

13 Stack the hairs to level the tips. Tie the bunch in on top of the hook shank to form the tail.

14 Trim off the butt ends of the moose hair and tidy with a few wraps of tying thread.

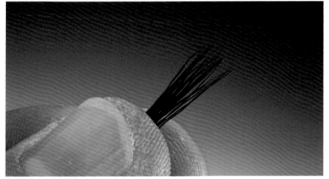

15 Take another small bunch of moose body hair. Clean and stack in a hair stacker.

16 Trim off the tips of the bunch as shown.

17 Tie in the bunch of moose body hair with the trimmed tips on top of the hook shank. Keep these hairs long so they are easier to separate from the tail hairs later.

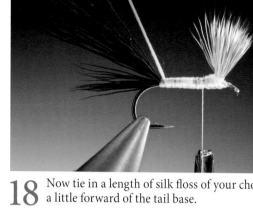

18 Now tie in a length of silk floss of your chosen color, a little forward of the tail base.

19 Wrap the floss forward and back to form the underbody. Finish the floss body at the wing base. Secure with a few turns of tying thread and remove any floss that is left.

20 Now, keeping the moose hairs parallel and taking care that they don't cross each other, pull them tightly over the floss underbody and secure with a few turns of tying thread.

21 Secure further as shown, slightly behind the wings, keeping all the hairs on top of the hook shank inbetween the wings. Take care that the moose hair overbody is balanced on each side of the underbody.

22 Select and prepare two hackles of the correct size: one brown, one grizzly.

23 Trim away the moose hair butt ends and tie down with a few more wraps of tying thread. Tie in the two hackles as shown at the overbody's finishing point.

24 Wrap your hackles one at a time. When wrapping the first hackle, leave a little space inbetween each turn so you have room to wrap the second hackle. The hackle on a Humpy should be as dense as possible.

25 Tie off the hackles, trim away the excess, whip finish, and place a small drop of varnish on the head.

Continued on page 94

26 The finished Humpy seen from below.

27 The finished Humpy seen from the side.

9

CDC Para-weld Mayfly

Making a para-weld post • CDC parachute hackling • Quilling tips

There are many different parachute hackling techniques, some traditional and some more modern, but very few use CDC.

Because of the unique floating and aero-dynamic qualities of CDC, I was looking to develop a parachute hackle that would resemble, perform and retain a comparable presentation to a traditional parachute hackle.

My initial objective was to avoid having to wrap the spun CDC dubbing brush around and under the thorax of the fly, which would later have to be trimmed on the underside. Although patterns adopting this technique perform adequately when fished, presentation is delivered somewhat higher, lifting the thorax out of the surface film of the water.

I wanted a technique that would not interfere with the abdomen and thorax of the pattern, giving an interested fish an uninterrupted view of the underside of the fly, yet suspending the whole body and thorax horizontally in the surface film.

This CDC para-weld tying technique is also an excellent choice for patterns representing other insects that are not up-winged, such as caddis, stone flies, ants, grasshoppers, and Klinkhamer-style emergers.

The polypropylene used for the post in this technique requires a test before use. I found several of the polypropylene yarns I tried troublesome. They burned, wouldn't melt at a low temperature, or lost their color when melted. So do a little heat test with the different polypropylene yarns you are planning to use, before you start.

The color of the polypropylene yarn used is entirely up to you. You can choose one to match the color of the wing or the body of the pattern being tied, or one as vibrant and visible as possible, which would double as a quick sight indicator for low light conditions or on broken water.

You may find that using a gallows tool helps to hold the polypropylene post in place while you wrap the CDC dubbing loop but, with a little practice, it can be wound just as easily without.

The spun CDC dubbing loop should be wound like a para-loop hackle from the base of the post around and upwards, until half of the dubbing loop has been used, and then wound down over the previous turns, finishing at the base of the post, tight into the thorax.

One advantage to this style of CDC parachute hackle is that it gives an extremely flexible hackle which will collapse under resistant air pressure when casting, but correct itself on landing back to its original shape and provide a very stable and level flotation element for the fly.

Another advantage with using a CDC fiber spun dubbing brush is that, when tying a traditional hackled parachute fly, the hackle size is matched to the hook size. But with this technique the fibers from the CDC dubbing brush can be trimmed to match any hook size from #6 all the way down to the smallest hooks. This means the time used for hackle scrutiny and selection is eliminated.

The hackle can also be made as sparse or dense as desired. If a sparse hackle is required, use only one side of a CDC hackle. If a more dense, more buoyant hackle is appropriate for the pattern being tied, use

TECHNIQUES MASTERED

- **Stripped quill body**
  Underbody preparation and wrapping of a tapered stripped peacock quill body.

- **CDC parachute hackle**
  How to prepare, spin and wrap a CDC dubbing brush parachute hackle for the para-weld technique.

- **Making a para-weld post**
  Correct polypropylene yarn selection and weld technique for the tying a para-weld wing.

two or more CDC hackles in the dubbing loop. If you would like a specific hackle color or shade, you can combine different or contrasting colors, or even ice dubbing or another flash material, to achieve the desired effect.

The resulting technique was inspired by a long working relationship with my good friend, and master of tying with CDC, Marc Petitjean.

Tying the CDC Para-weld Mayfly

THE DRESSING

Hook: Mustad R30 #10-16
Thread: Your choice of color
Tail: Coq de Leon
Post: Polypropylene yarn
Body: Stripped peacock herl or moose mane hairs
Thorax: Dubbing or peacock herl
Hackle: One or more CDC hackles

WATCH THE VIDEOS

youtu.be/DaNOD1RZAx0
Tying the CDC Para-weld Mayfly with Barry Ord Clarke

youtu.be/ShuWsnX17jk
Magic Tool tutorial with Barry Ord Clarke

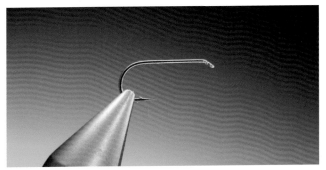

1   Secure your dry fly hook in the vise, as shown, with the hook shank horizontal.

2   Run a fine foundation of tying thread along two-thirds of the hook shank.

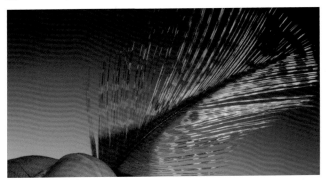

3   Select a nicely marked Coq de Leon hackle for the tail fibers.

4   Take a small bunch of Coq de Leon fibers for the tail and tie in on top of the hook shank. This is important to allow the hook bend to sink under the surface! The tail should be approximately the same length as the hook shank.

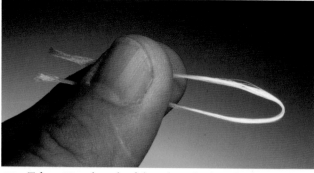

5 Take a 10cm length of the selected color of polypropylene yarn you wish to use for the post weld, as shown.

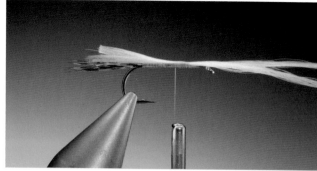

6 Tie in the poly loop at the correct position for the post.

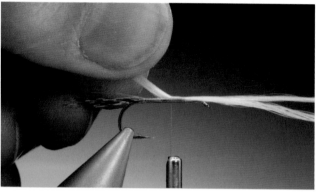

7 Make sure that you have enough poly yarn at the rear of the post to hold.

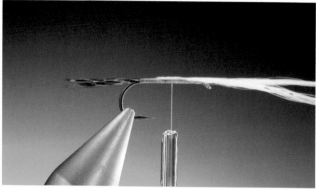

8 Trim off the ends of the poly yarn at a slight angle, so that when covered with tying thread they create a tapered body.

9 Even up the body with tying thread to a slight taper. Make a few turns with tying thread tight into the front of the post, so it rises 90 degrees from the hook shank.

10 Select your desired color of stripped quill.

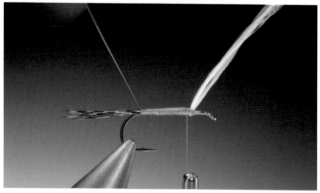

11 Tie in a stripped quill, by the thinest end, at the base of the tail, ready for wrapping.

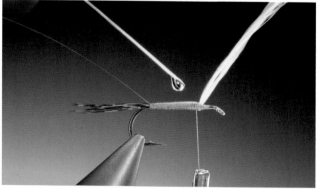

12 If you would like to make the quill body a little more robust, give the underbody a fine coat with varnish or superglue, before you wrap the quill.

13 Wrap the quill in even, neat, tight turns all the way up to the thorax. Tie off.

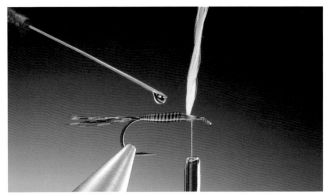

14 If desired, use a dubbing needle to apply only a thin coat of UV resin, to protect the quill.

15 At the base of the post, make a 12cm-long dubbing loop.

16 Apply a little dubbing to the tying thread and make two or three turns behind the dubbing loop.

17 Load one or two CDC hackles in a Magic Clip, as shown, and cut away the hackle stems.

18 Dub the remaining thorax and make a whip finish. Place the CDC clip in the dubbing loop and spin to form a dubbing brush.

19 Now wrap about half the CDC dubbing brush up the poly post. If you have a gallows tool to hold the post in position, you may find this helpful.

20 Once you have wound the CDC dubbing brush halfway up the post, wind it down again into the thorax as shown.

21 Holding all the CDC away from the hook eye, bring the remainder of the dubbing loop round and over the hook eye. Secure with a couple of loose turns of tying thread.

22 Once held in position, pull the remainder of the dubbing loop tight to straighten up the wing. Once tight, trim off the excess dubbing loop, tie off, and whip finish.

23 Remove your tying thread. Holding the poly post in one hand, push down the CDC fibers so that they are more compact and closer to the thorax. Here I am using the notch on a Petitjean stacker tool to do this.

24 Once the CDC para hackle is in position, trim off the poly post about 1cm above the hackle.

25 Now take a cauterizing tool and carefully melt the poly post gradually down into the CDC hackle. Take your time with this and try not to burn it.

26 Once melted correctly, the poly yarn will weld the hackle in place and form a neat even bead, on top of the hackle center.

27 Now with your left hand, push all the CDC fibers trapped between your finger and thumb upwards. Once you have them in the correct position, trim off the CDC ends.

28 Once done, the hackle will fall back into position when released. The hackle should now be the correct diameter and it should be even all the way round. If the hackle diameter is too large, repeat step 27, and trim off a little more.

29 View from below with the exposed abdomen and thorax.

30 The finished para-weld and quick-sight poly bead on top.

Additional technique for a Sparkle Wing

1 Select your preferred color of ice dubbing.

2 Place a sparse amount of dubbing over the jaws of the Petitjean Table Clip.

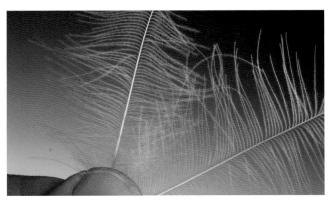

3 Select one or even two different colored CDC hackles.

4 Load the Table Clip with the CDC hackles over the ice dubbing.

5 Transfer the CDC and ice dubbing to a Magic Clip.

6 Load the dubbing loop with the Clip and spin into a dubbing brush. Before you start wrapping the hackle, give it a brush to release any trapped fibers.

7 Complete as the CDC para-weld hackle above for the finished sparkle wing. This is it viewed from above.

8 The finished sparkle wing from below.
You can also trim the wing to shape for an excellent spent spinner wing.

Detached Deer Hair Body Mayfly

Making the detached mayfly body • Partridge feather legs

This pattern demonstrates the extreme versatility of deer hair, in which it is used in three different techniques to construct the tail, the extended body and the wing.

It is a pattern I have been tying for years to imitate the larger species of my local mayflies, *vulgata* and *danica*, but it can easily be adapted, not only for other mayflies but also for daddy-long-legs' bodies, just by changing the body size and color of the deer hair.

It's not essential that you have a upholsterer's needle to tie the extended body: you can use a tube fly tool or just a regular sewing needle, but these lack that finished natural curved body effect.

If you are going to purchase a upholsterer's needle, make sure that you buy one that has a round profile on both the shank and the point. If you try to use one that has a flat spearhead point, it will make removing the body when finished, difficult.

In addition to the upholsterer's needle, another helpful item to have to hand is a short plastic tube. I am sure that if you take a look around your tying bench or have a rummage amongst your tying tools, you'll find a plastic tube of some description or another.

If you have seen many of my tying tutorials, you will know that I often use plastic tubes, in various sizes and forms, to make many tying procedures easier to execute. This is one of those occasions.

Plastic tubes (*see below*) are a helpful little addition to the tying bench. I always keep a good selection of twenty or so tubes of various sizes close to hand. These have not been bought but collected and saved every time I have come across one that could be useful.

I use them for many jobs such as setting reverse hackles and Wally Wings, forming perfect heads on Thunder Creek streamers, and for Madam X and other bullet head dry flies, to name only a few.

I prefer using clear plastic tubes for jobs such as the one I demonstrate here. It enables the tyer to actually see what is going on within the tube when placed over the material to hold it in position. This way the fly tyer has full control over the position of each hair before beginning to make the first wraps of tying thread.

TECHNIQUES MASTERED

- **Making a detached mayfly body**
  Needle in vise technique for making extremely buoyant, elongated, detached deer hair bodies for mayflies.

- **Partridge hackle legs**
  Using the traditional speckled partridge hackle tying technique to create mayfly legs.

- **Down wing of deer hair**
  Method for tying a front-mounted down wing of deer hair.

Tying the Detached Deer Hair Body Mayfly

THE DRESSING

Hook: Mustad C49 #10-16
Thread: Dyneema and olive tying thread
Tail: Moose body hair
Body: Olive deer hair
Thorax: Olive super-fine dubbing
Hackle: Olive dyed speckled partridge
Wing: Golden olive deer hair

WATCH THE VIDEO

https://youtu.be/xWu_Y7hmnMI

Tying the Detached Deer Hair Body Mayfly
with Barry Ord Clarke

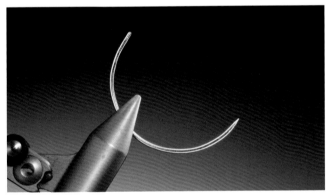

1 Secure your upholsterer's needle in the jaws of your vise, as shown.

2 Coat the point and body of the needle with a little tacky tying wax.

3 Using Dyneema or GSP thread makes tying this pattern easier.

4 Once you have attached your tying thread, spin your bobbin anti-clockwise to give it a flat profile. Run a fine foundation of tying thread over the waxed part of the needle. Don't wrap this too tight, otherwise you'll not be able to remove the body later!

5 Select two or three straight moose body hairs for the tail. Some of the absolute best moose and deer hair products come from Nature's Spirit.

6 Tie these in on top of the needle. The tail should be approximately the same length as the body.

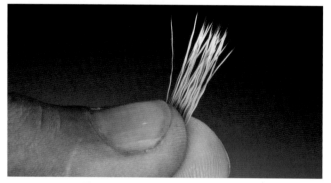

7 Cut a small bunch of olive deer hair, about the thickness of a matchstick. Remove all the underfur and shorter hairs and stack in a hair stacker.

8 Tie the bunch of deer hair on the needle as shown, a little down from the point. Take care that the hairs are evenly distributed round the needle. Now make a few careful wraps of tying thread around the needle towards the needle point, and back down again.

9 Carefully fold back the olive deer hair, to reveal the tail.

10 Using a plastic tube, push the body hair down over the needle.

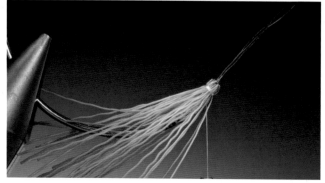

11 While the tube is still in position, make the first body segment wraps. Remove the tube.

12 With a waterproof felt pen, color just enough of your tying thread to make a few wraps to mark the segment.

13 Now use the next un-colored section of tying thread to make the first wraps of the next body segment before you color it again. This will keep each diagonal wrap of tying thread that moves you down to each body segment, less visible. Repeat.

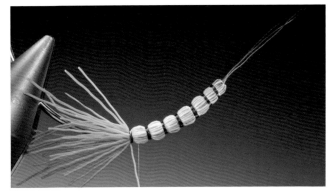

14 Continue tying the segmentation along the whole body.

15 Once you have completed the whole body, whip finish on the last segment and remove your tying thread. You can, if you wish, give the wrappings of each segment a fine coat of UV resin or varnish to strengthen them.

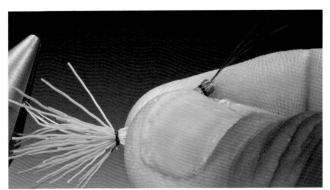

16 Grip the body carefully and gently twist and pull at the same time to release the body from the needle.

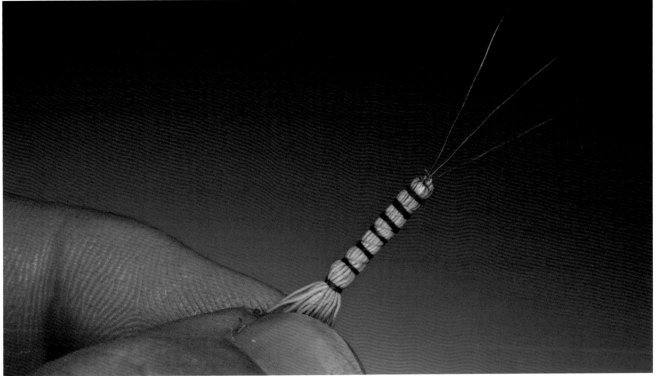

17 Once removed, you can place a tiny drop of UV resin inbetween the base of tail hairs to keep them fanned out.

18 Now secure your hook in the vise and attach a short foundation of regular olive tying thread.

19 Dub a little olive super-fine dubbing as shown. This will stop the deer hair body from slipping when attached.

20 Now tie on your deer hair body. Once the butt ends flare, run your tying thread forward through the hairs, securing it correctly.

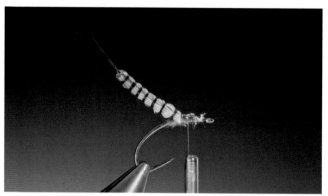

21 Once the body is correctly positioned and secure, trim away the remaining deer hair.

22 Take a little more super-fine olive dubbing and build a slender thorax.

23 Select and prepare an olive speckled partridge hackle as shown.

24 Tie the partridge hackle in by the tip, a little forward of the detached body.

25 Wrap the partridge hackle as shown, to form the mayfly legs, and tie off. *Continued page 112*

26 With a little more super-fine olive dubbing, cover the thorax.

27 Take a small bunch of the olive deer hair, remove all the underfur and shorter hairs. Even up the tips in a hair stacker.

28 Tie the bunch in on top of the thorax, about the same length as the body, and secure.

29 Trim away the butt ends of the wing to form the head of the fly and whip finish.

11

Deer Hair Irresistible

....

How to spin and clip deer hair body • Deer hair hackling

....

I created this variant of the great original Irresistible, just to illustrate the versatility of deer hair.

Here we have three types: deer hair, moose body hair and Comparadun deer hair—and three different techniques. The key to getting this pattern right is choosing the right deer hair for the right job.

First let's look at moose hair for making the tail. Moose body hair is straight, stiff, naturally black and has very fine tapered tips that make it ideal for mayfly tails. As with deer hair, moose body hair is made up of small air-filled cells. This contributes to the buoyancy of dry flies but, like deer hair, it will also flare when placed under pressure from the

tying thread. Unlike more stable hairs, a specific technique is required for tying in deer hair tails.

It's important that you have a short foundation of tying thread on the center hook shank, so the hair has a little more purchase and won't slip and slide around the hook. Cut, clean and stack a small bunch of moose body hair and secure with a couple of wraps of tying thread.

Now wrap your tying thread back towards the tail base with looser turns of thread, so you reduce the pressure on the hair from the tying thread, which in turn will reduce the flare and keep the tail nice and straight.

Once you are happy with the tail position, wind back up the hook shank, increasing pressure as you go.

To create the body of the Irresistible you will need a really strong tying thread and a heavy dubbing spinner.

In order to compress the deer hair tightly into a dense dubbing brush, I recommend that you use Dyneema or GSP tying thread. One of the few disadvantages of using Dyneema or GSP tying thread is that it's very slippery. If you don't use wax you may find that the dubbing loop spins above and below the deer hair, so that the hair gets pushed into one large clump, in the center of the loop. Once your dubbing brush is spun, it should resemble step 15.

Dyneema requires wax when spinning deer hair in a dubbing loop. Since the introduction of pre-waxed tying thread, tying wax is overlooked nowadays, so if you don't own any flytying wax, I recommend that you obtain some. You will find that when used correctly it will significantly improve and simplify many tying techniques and procedures.

Before you start wrapping the dubbing brush, you may want to place a small piece of masking tape over the moose body tail. This will make it easier to avoid accidentally cutting the tail when trimming the body.

When wrapping the deer hair dubbing brush, take care not to trap hairs from the previous wrap. Trapped hairs will make trimming the body to a nice finish difficult.

TECHNIQUES MASTERED

- **Moose hair tail**
  Correct method for tying a moose body hair dry fly tail that doesn't flare.

- **Spinning deer hair in a dubbing loop**
  How to prepare and spin deer hair in a dubbing loop to create spun and clipped deer hair bodies.

- **Deer hair hackle**
  Choosing and spinning deer hair in a dubbing loop to make a deer hair dry fly hackle.

Scissors with serrated blades are the best for trimming deer hair. Regular smooth blades tend to push some of the deer hair forward and out of the blades. The serrated edge has more purchase on the hair, which results in a clean cut.

For the deer hair hackle, I like to use shorter, stiffer summer or mid-season deer hair. This will work much better as a hackle when spun and wrapped.

When you are transferring the deer hair from the Magic Clip to the dubbing loop, try to have 2-3mm of the cut end in the dubbing loop. When spun, these won't be visible, but will support the finer, longer deer hair fibers.

Tying the Deer Hair Irresistible

THE DRESSING

Hook: Mustad R30 #10-14
Thread: Dyneema
Tail: Moose body hair
Body: Natural spinning deer hair
Hackle: Comparadun deer hair

WATCH THE VIDEO

youtu.be/kB8iKxFmgAQ

Tying the Deer Hair Irresistible with
Barry Ord Clarke

MAGIC TOOL VIDEO

youtu.be/ShuWsnX17jk

Magic Tool tutorial
with Barry Ord Clarke

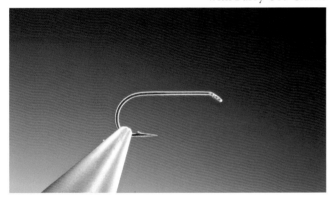

1   Secure your dry fly hook in the vise, as shown, with the hook shank horizontal.

2   Run a fine foundation of tying thread along the center of the hook shank.

3   Select a small bunch of moose body hair for the tail.

4   Place the moose body hair in a hair stacker and even out the tips.

5 The tail should be approximately the same length as the hook shank. Tie in the bunch on top of the hook shank. Take care not to use too tight wraps of tying thread as this will flare the moose body hair.

6 Once secure you can now wind your tying thread forward with tighter turns as you go.

7 Trim off the excess moose body hair and finish with a few wraps of tying thread.

8 Take a short strip of deer hair. Make sure that the strip is not too thick.

9 Place the strip in a Magic Clip and, with straight long scissors, cut away the strip of hide.

10 Using another Clip, reverse the tips of deer hair, so they are on the outside of the Clip.

11 Trim off the tips as shown.

12 Make a 10cm-long dubbing loop at the rear of the hook shank.

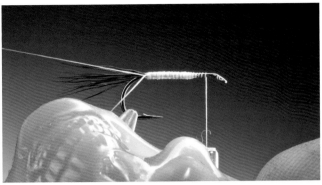

13 If you are using Dyneema, run a little tying wax over the loop. This will stop the deer hair from slipping.

14 Load the dubbing loop with the deer hair. If it's a little thick in some places, just thin it out by sliding the hair down the dubbing loop, but keeping it even.

15 Using a heavy dubbing spinner, spin the dubbing loop until it is even and tight.

16 Now wrap your deer hair dubbing brush forward, taking care to brush the hair back with your left hand after each turn.

17 Once you have covered the whole hook shank, tie off behind the hook eye. Whip finish.

18 Remove your tying thread and, using a hair packer, push the spun deer hair body back. This will pack the hair a little tighter.

19 Use a pair of serrated scissors if you have them to shape the body. Control the tail hairs with your left hand, while you trim the body with your right.

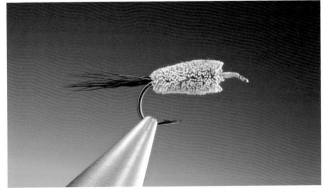

20 Take your time trimming the body until the desired shape and size is achieved.

21 For the deer hair hackle you will need some short stiff deer hair. Comparadun hair works well for this.

22 Re-attach your tying thread behind the hook eye.

23 Now make another dubbing loop, this time a little shorter than the one for the body.

24 Load another Clip with the hackle hair. The tips of the hair should remain on the inside of the Clip for this dubbing loop.

25 Wax your Dyneema tying thread.

26 Place the deer hair in the dubbing loop and spin into a tight dubbing brush.

27 Wrap the deer hair hackle forward, once again brushing back the fibers with each turn. Tie off.

28 Whip finish and remove your tying thread. Position the deer hair hackle.

12

Large Mayfly Dun

Split flank winging • Double collar hackling • Moose mane body

This Large Mayfly Dun has saved the day for me many a time, especially during prolific hatches, when the fish have been very selective. If you adjust the position of the wings straight out from each side of the hook shank, you couldn't have a better candidate for fishing an evening spent spinner fall.

Carefully selecting the moose mane hairs for the body will give you the opportunity to customize your bodies (*see Wally Wing Dun page 81*).

These create the most realistic mayfly bodies and are surprisingly robust, even when matched up against the small sharp teeth of trout. But if in doubt, you can always give the body a fine coat of head cement or UV resin.

When wrapping the moose mane hairs, care should be taken that they are held parallel and not twisted or crossed over each other, while wrapping. If done correctly, this technique can be used to make beautiful tapered, segmented bodies, not only for mayflies but also midges.

The classic vertical split flank wing is representative of many dry flies including the famous Catskill patterns and this iconic winging style was standard on many of the classic American dry flies.

The original material for tying a flank feather dry fly wing is lemon wood duck flank. These barred lemon flank feathers are not cheap and in recent years have become a little more difficult to obtain in reasonable quality.

An accepted substitute can be achieved by skillful dying of barred mallard flank taken from where the "silver" flank feathers are just starting to shade into

the "bronze" shoulder plumage. Some substitutes offered for sale are less than successful.

There are many ways to tie these wings, but on the larger patterns I find this method quick and easy.

The reason for choosing furnace hackles on this pattern was to continue to match the color scheme throughout, from tail to wing tip, for the *vulgata* mayfly. But change the moose mane body hair and wing color to match your hatch.

TECHNIQUES MASTERED

● **Match the hatch body**
Mixing different colored moose mane hairs to create ultra-realistic mayfly "quill" bodies.

● **Split flank wings**
Simple method for mounting split dyed mallard flank dry fly wings.

● **Double collar hackle**
Technique for using two cock hackles instead of one on large patterns, to increase hackle density.

Tying the Large Mayfly Dun

THE DRESSING

Hook: Mustad C53S #8-12
Thread: Tan
Tail: Moose body hairs
Body: Moose mane hairs
Wings: Lemon wood duck
    or mallard drake flank
Thorax: Cream super-fine dubbing
Hackle: Two furnace hackles

WATCH THE VIDEO

youtu.be/ExDkZDUjvEY

Tying the Mayfly Dun
with Barry Ord Clarke

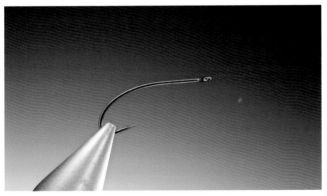

1   Secure your dry fly hook in the vise, as shown, with the hook shank horizontal.

2   Run a fine foundation of tying thread along the center of the hook shank.

3   Take the small bunch of moose body hair for the tail, even up the tips in a hair stacker and tie in on top of the hook shank. This is important to allow the hook bend to sink under the surface. The tail should be approximately the same length as the hook shank.

4   Once secure, run your tying thread under the hair and up about two-thirds of the hook shank, as shown.

5 Now make a few turns of tying thread around the hair. This will hold it in place while you finish the underbody.

6 You can now cover the whole body with a foundation of tying thread. Make one turn of tying thread under the tail to support it.

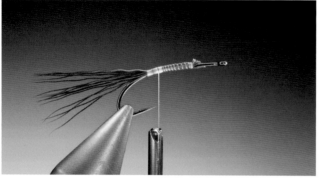

7 Trim off the ends of the moose body hair.

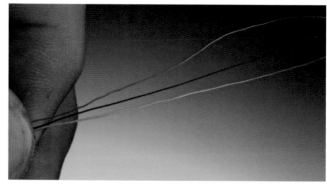

8 Select three long moose mane hairs: two with brown tips and one black.

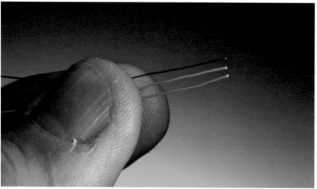

9 Holding the tips of the three moose mane hairs level, trim off the butt ends so all the hairs are the same length.

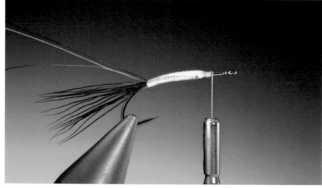

10 Tie in the three hairs by the tips. Make sure that all three hair tips are close to each other. Build up a slight taper along the body, finishing with your tying thread a little behind the hook eye.

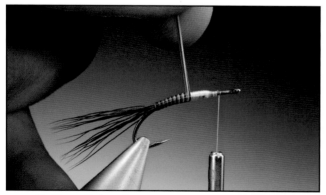

11 Holding all three hairs at once, carefully wrap them in tight, neat turns up over the body. Take care not to twist or cross the hairs over each other.

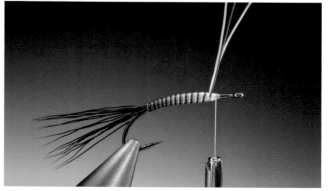

12 Once the whole body is complete, tie off the hairs at the thorax. You should have a nice segmented body effect.

13 Select two mallard drake flank feathers, natural or dyed. Pull all the fibers together to form a wing.

14 Tie in the mallard flank as shown for the first wing. This should be approximately the same length as the body.

15 Repeat for the second wing.

16 Select two furnace or silver badger hackles of the correct size for the hook.

17 Tie in the two hackles side by side at the rear of the thorax, close in to the moose mane body.

18 Spin a little cream super-fine dubbing onto your tying thread and cover the thorax.

19 Catch both the hackles in a hackle plier and wind forward. Tie off behind the hook eye.

20 Secure the hackles, cut away the excess and whip finish. Remove your tying thread, and varnish.

21 You can now trim away all the hackle fibers on the underside of the thorax. Here is the finished fly.

13

CDC Mayfly Spinner

Spent CDC wings • Twist & wrap CDC body • Upside-down tying

This mayfly spent spinner pattern demonstrates four very different techniques with CDC. Once learned and mastered, all four techniques can be adapted and applied to many other patterns.

CDC feathers come from the preen gland of a duck. Natural untreated and undyed CDC from wild ducks have by far the best water-repellent qualities. These feathers retain the natural oils.

The majority of the CDC that is available to the tyer is from domestic duck stock, bred for the meat industry. These vary in quality, because some producers use dying techniques which remove so much of the natural oils that they then have to treat them, after dying, with silicone to make them float! But there are reliable sources of CDC out there.

As with all other natural materials, quality CDC is paramount if optimal results are to be achieved. For this Mayfly Spinner, large CDC hackles are required to make the extra-long body and the wide, spread, spent mayfly wing.

Before you start using your CDC, I recommend getting hold of a plastic box: a large ice-cream box will do. Take the whole packet of CDC and empty it all into the box—this way you can easily separate the feathers according to size and quality. Once you have categorized them into small ziplock bags, locating the required size of hackle is quick and easy, substantially reducing tying time.

If we start with the rear body section of the spent spinner, this is made from a CDC dubbing brush. When such a small area is to be dubbed, the smaller, inferior-quality CDC hackles can be used, using the micro or small Magic Tool. If these hackles are sparse in fiber count, use several to increase the density of the dubbing brush.

For the main body of the abdomen, a larger CDC hackle is required. This hackle should also have longer fibers, as these help accomplish a successful segmented body, with the twist and wrap technique.

The wing case is more or less straightforward. Here we need one, two or three medium CDC hackles of a similar size. Place the first hackle, concave side down, on the table. Follow this with the second and third hackle, so all three hackle tips are level. Pick up all three hackles together by the stems, and tie in on the thorax, concave side down. This will give you a natural curve when folded over the thorax, to form the wing case.

When making the spent wing dubbing brush, mixing two or more differently colored CDC hackles gives you the opportunity to customize the wings, from a subtle nuance to a bold color.

You can also put some ice dubbing in the mix for an excellent sparkle wing effect *(see page 103)*.

To achieve the correct wing shape, care should be taken when choosing the CDC hackles. Once you have drawn the CDC fibers of each hackle 90 degrees from the hackle stem, ready for loading the Magic Tool, each hackle should slightly resemble a

TECHNIQUES MASTERED

- **Twist and wrap CDC body**
  Technique for using CDC hackles to create very buoyant and slender CDC segmented bodies.

- **CDC wing case**
  How to use one or more CDC hackles to great effect as spent wing dividers and wing cases.

- **CDC spent wings**
  Spinning one or more CDC hackles in various colors in a dubbing loop to create perfect spent wings.

Christmas tree with the shortest hackle fibers at the top of the stem, getting longer towards the bottom.

Load into the Magic Clip, ready for the dubbing loop: one end of the CDC fibers should be short and the other end long. When placed in the dubbing loop, the long side should be closest the table.

Doing this will result in the correct wing shape when spun and wrapped.

Tying the CDC Mayfly Spinner

THE DRESSING

Hook: Mustad C53S #10-14
Thread: Beige or tan
Tail: Coq de Leon
Body: Beige and cream CDC
Wing case: Two or three small beige CDC hackles
Wing: Three large CDC hackles white, cream, and blue dun

WATCH THE VIDEO

youtu.be/61cc6VFUt_M

Tying the CDC Mayfly Spinner with Barry Ord Clarke

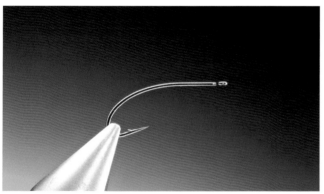

1   Secure your dry fly hook in the vise, as shown, with the hook shank horizontal.

2   Run a fine foundation of tying thread along the length of the hook shank.

3   Select a nicely marked Coq de Leon hackle for the tail fibers.

4   Take a small bunch of Coq de Leon fibers for the tail and tie in on top of the hook shank, pointing downwards. The tail should be approximately the same length as the hook shank.

5 Run a foundation of tying thread over the whole hook shank, forming a slight taper.

6 Load a Magic Clip with a single short beige CDC hackle.

7 Wrap your tying thread back down to the tail base and split your tying thread. Insert the CDC between the threads and spin into a dubbing brush.

8 Wrap the dubbing brush tightly at the tail base.

9 Select a single, cream-colored CDC hackle.

10 With two loose turns of tying thread, attach the CDC hackle to the hook shank. Carefully pull the CDC hackle through the loose turns of thread until the tip fibers are shorter than the hook shank. Tie down, keeping your tying thread forward on the hook.

11 Attach a hackle plier to the end of the CDC hackle. Now twist the CDC hackle as you wrap forward and form the segmented body.

12 When you reach the tying thread, tie off the CDC and trim away the excess stem.

13 Now give the whole body a good brushing.

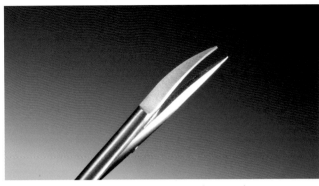

14 The next stage is made easier with curved scissors.

15 Trim away all the CDC fibers from the body. The result should be a cream abdomen with a dark beige base.

16 Rotate your vise. Select two or three beige CDC hackles and align them on top of each other. Tie these in on top of the hook shank tight into the abdomen, as shown.

17 Trim off the excess CDC hackle stems and tidy up with a few wraps of tying thread.

18 Now you'll need three large CDC hackles: white, cream and blue dun.

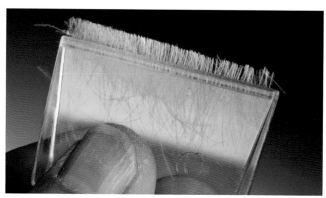

19 Load all three CDC hackles into a Magic Clip.

20 Split your tying thread to form a dubbing loop. Insert the CDC in the dubbing loop with the longest fibers in the lower part of the loop, and spin to form a dubbing brush.

21 Now wrap the dubbing brush, taking care to smooth the fibers back with each turn over the whole thorax. Tie off behind the hook eye.

22 Separate the CDC fibers out to the sides, into two equal-sized wings.

Continued page 136

23 Collect all the beige CDC hackles, taking care not to twist them, so the fibers lie parallel. Fold these over the thorax to form the wing case and tie down.

24 Trim away the remaining CDC stems and whip finish.

25 Remove your tying thread and place a small drop of varnish on the head. Trim your wings to shape.

26 Your finished CDC Mayfly Spinner.

14

All Hackle Dry

Splayed Coq de Leon hackling • Reverse parachute • Antron tailing

This is a technique that I recently developed for making very simple, flared, reverse parachute-style hackles from all types of feathers, not just cock hackles.

The technique allows you to develop unique hackles from all manner of feathers: partridge, teal, mallard, Coq de Leon; whatever you fancy using.

The only requirement is that the hackle fibers have a little rigidity to them.

You can also use this technique to make hair hackles with squirrel tail, deer hair and badger.

The yarn should be fine and sparse. A polypropylene yarn floats better than Antron, but both work.

Whatever you choose it should be tied in on top of the hook shank, just a little down the bend of the hook, with all its fibers as close and tight as possible.

The fibers that you decide to use have to be stacked first in a hair stacker to level all the tips, otherwise the finished flared hackle will not be circular.

As with other parachute patterns that I tie and fish with, I like to dress them with a slightly larger hackle than the norm, for the hook size I am using. Measuring the length of the fibers will also determine the size (circumference) of the hackle.

Care should be taken when tying in the fibers, rather like a tail, in over the floss. They must be kept central on top of the hook shank.

If they slip around, down the sides, or under the hook shank, they will flare in all directions, or not at all, when split with the yarn.

The thorax is also reversed so the peacock herl has to be tied in by the tip in such a way that when wrapped, the flue length increases in size, creating a tapered thorax.

The pearl tinsel is not necessary: you can also use dubbing or whatever else works for you, but I have found this body is excellent for imitating hatching midges and the smaller mayflies such as *Leptophlebia*.

For mayflies I keep the tail and I dispense with it for midges.

This technique lends itself to the use of many types of hackle: teal, mallard, partridge and Coq de Leon, in all its colors. Even golden pheasant tippet works, but those that are a little stiffer tend to work best.

When tying in the barbs from your chosen hackle type, try to keep the tips as even as possible. A hair stacker will give the best, most even results.

Tie the bunch in as you would any traditional dry fly tail. Remember the proportion: double the length of tail will determine the final hackle diameter.

Another advantage with this method is that if you start with a barb length of, let's say, 1.5cm, which is the perfect hackle size for a size 8 hook, you can tie these in shorter, to produce the correct hackle size for smaller hook sizes. A kind of "one size fits all." This means that the time wasted on hackle scrutiny and selection is eliminated.

Tying the All Hackle Dry

THE DRESSING

Hook: Mustad C53S #10-16
Thread: Black
Hackle: Coq de Leon
Tail: Antron or polypropylene yarn
Wing case: Antron or polypropylene yarn
Thorax: Peacock herl
Body: Pearl tinsel
Rib: Tying thread

WATCH THE VIDEO

youtu.be/5MenKBVGv7g
Tying the All Hackle Dry with
Barry Ord Clarke

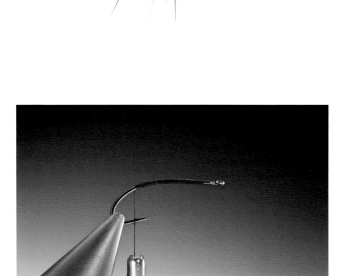

1 Secure your dry fly hook in the vise as shown, with the hook eye pointing a little downwards. This will help tying in the yarn and hackle fibers.

2 Run a fine foundation of tying thread along two-thirds of the hook shank.

3 Cut a length of Antron or poly yarn and tie this in as shown. Take care to keep the yarn on top of the hook shank.

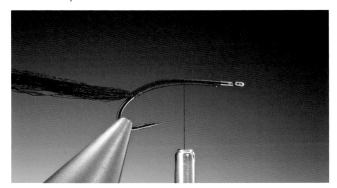

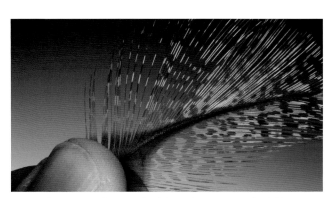

4 Select a Coq de Leon hackle with nicely marked fibers.

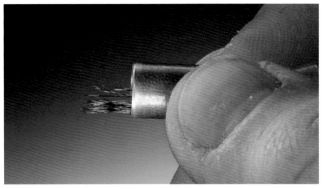

5 Take a bunch of Coq de Leon fibers for the hackle and stack in a hair stacker, so the tips are level.

6 Tie the fibers in on top of the hook shank, over the yarn. The length of the fibers should be determined by the size of your hook.

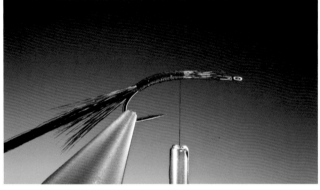

7 If the Coq de Leon fibers are too long, trim them off at an angle.

8 Give the whole body a smooth foundation of tying thread.

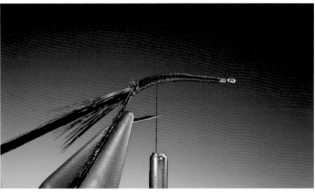

9 Tie in one or two peacock herls tight into the hackle fibers.

10 Before you wind your peacock herl, make 10 to 12 open wraps of tying thread forward towards the hook eye.

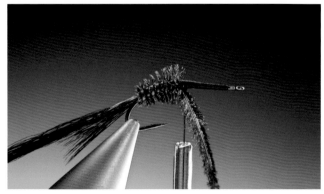

11 Attach a hackle plier to the peacock herl and rotate your vise. If you don't have a full-rotary vise, wrap as normal, to form the thorax. Tie off the peacock herl.

12 Cut a length of pearl tinsel.

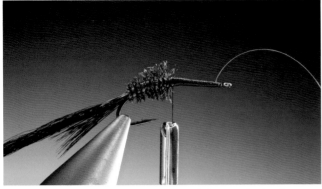

13 Tie in the length of pearl tinsel close to the hook eye, and then wind your thread back towards the thorax.

14 Wrap the pearl tinsel back towards the thorax and tie off. Remove the excess tinsel.

15 Take hold of the yarn and lift in order to separate the hackle fibers in half. Fold over the yarn and secure with two loose turns of tying thread at the rear of the thorax. Pull on the yarn to tighten and splay the fibers into a hackle.

16 Now rib the body with even, open turns of tying thread and tie off the yarn at the hook eye. Whip finish.

17 Separate the tail yarn, make another whip finish and remove the tying thread.

18 Trim the tails to the required length, and give the head a little varnish. The finished fly viewed from above.

19 The finished fly viewed from below.

20 Viewed from the side.

15

House Builder Caddis

Making the caddis larva head • Spider-style hackling • Herl bodywork

This pattern imitates the aquatic larval stage of the House Builder Caddis fly, and is one of the most important foods for trout and grayling, especially during the late autumn and winter.

Caddis flies are closely related to terrestrial moths, including the silkworm moth. The caddis fly larvae use silk as an adhesive to build elaborate mobile homes from twigs, vegetation, gravel, and just about anything else that is readily available, to camouflage and protect their soft vulnerable bodies.

In fast-flowing rivers they will also use small stones to act as extra weight and anchorage. The materials for these houses are cemented together with a fine silk that they produce with the help of a gland in the larva's mouth.

Interestingly enough, the English name "caddis" can be traced back as far as 1611 to William Shakespeare's *The Winter's Tale* where Shakespeare writes about the Caddysses man. This was a street merchant who sold fine silk, textiles and haberdashery. These salesmen dressed in overcoats which were covered with small patches of different textiles, from head to toe, to show their wares!

Bakewell in Derbyshire where I lived for some years is the home of the famous river Wye. Where the river runs past an engineering workshop, armored caddis larvae can be found!

Here the caddis fly larvae make their houses from the small twisted aluminum burrs that have been discarded and find their way into the river.

The cased caddis larvae are mobile foragers, their head and legs exposed as they pull their houses around with them.

Peacock herl bodies as used in this fly can be a little vulnerable, but you can reinforce your herl bodies. Tie in a length of wire with the peacock herl. Before you begin to wrap your herl, give the underbody a fine coat with super glue, wrap your herl over the superglue and secure behind the hook eye. Then wrap the wire as a rib, in the opposite direction, over the herl and tie off.

If you require even more weight for fishing deep pools in fast-flowing water, you can add extra weight with the addition of more lead wire on the underbody, but you can also replace the UV resin head with a heavy Tungsten bead.

This requires a little technique for attaching it at the bend of the hook. Take a short length of heavy gauge mono-filament, make sure that it fits snugly through your chosen bead size and melt one end of the mono with a lighter.

Thread your bead on the mono, and the melted end will function as a stop. Now tie the mono to the hook shank. Once secured in the correct position, proceed as normal.

- **Caddis larva head & body**
  Creating a caddis larva head with tying thread and UV resin and the soft creamy protruding body parts.

- **Spider-style legs**
  Selection and preparation of a speckled partridge hackle for a classic spider-legs effect.

- **Herl body**
  Under- and overbody preparation for a chunky tapered peacock herl cased caddis body.

English partridge along with pheasant tail, peacock herl and hare's ear, is one of the quintessential flytying materials for trout and grayling patterns. When buying partridge, I suggest that you look at full skins, unless you only need a small amount of dyed partridge, in which case packets of loose hackles are more economical. A full skin will give you the broadest amount of choice of color and hackle size.

Tying the House Builder Caddis

THE DRESSING

Hook: Mustad R75 #10-16
Thread: Black
Head: Tying thread and UV resin
Legs: Speckled partridge hackle
Body: Ostrich herl
Cased body: Peacock herl

WATCH THE VIDEO

youtu.be/h_uMdOto4_A

Tying the House Builder Caddis
Larva with Barry Ord Clarke

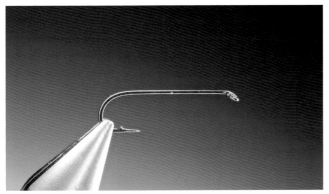

1 Secure your streamer hook in the vise, as shown, with the hook shank horizontal.

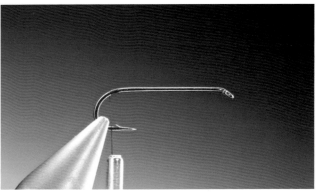

2 Attach the tying thread at the rear of the hook shank.

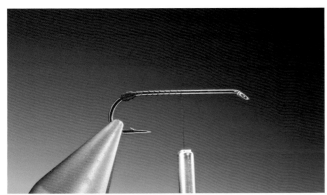

3 Make a small ball of tying thread, just above the hook barb, then wind the tying thread about halfway up the hook shank in open spiral turns.

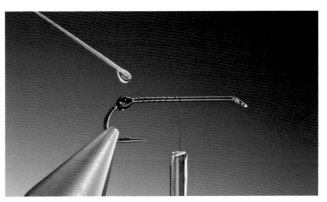

4 Give the head a coat with UV resin.

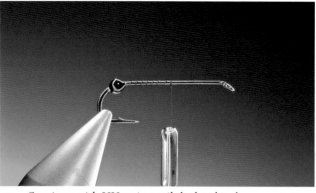

5 Continue with UV resin until the head is the correct size.

6 Select a well-marked brown speckled partridge hackle.

7 To prepare the partridge hackle, attach a hackle plier to the point and pull the shaft fibers 90 degrees to the hackle stem.

8 Pull the fibers from one side of the hackle, as shown, taking care not to damage the tip or the remaining fibers on the opposite side.

9 Tie in the hackle by the tip at a slight angle as shown, directly behind the head of the caddis larva.

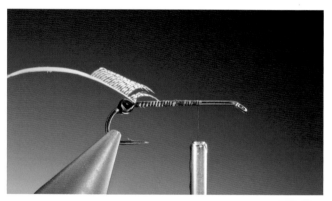

10 Cut away the excess tip of the partridge hackle and secure with a few wraps of tying thread.

11 Attach a hackle plier to the stem of the partridge hackle and wrap the hackle as shown. Tie off with a few turns of tying thread.

12 Select a good-quality cream or natural ostrich herl.

13 Tie in the herl at the rear of the partridge hackle.

14 Make seven or eight turns of herl to form the caddis larva's fleshy body. Tie off the herl.

15 Trim away the excess herl.

16 Take some small, medium or large-size lead wire, depending on your hook size.

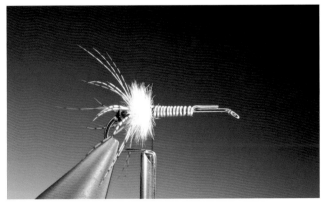

17 Considering how much weight you require, make a few wraps of lead wire from behind the larva body.

18 Cover the wraps of lead wire with tying thread as shown. Keep your tying thread hanging between the lead wire and the hook eye.

19 Select two to five peacock herl fibers, depending on hook size. Lay these down on top of the hook shank, over the lead wire, and secure all the way into the ostrich herl body.

20 Wind your tying thread back to the hook eye. Take hold of all the peacock herls at once, being careful not to twist them together! Now wrap them forward towards the hook eye, keeping each wrap tight into the last. Tie off behind the hook eye.

21 Remove the excess peacock herl and whip finish. Remove your tying thread and coat the whippings with a little head cement.

22 The finished House Builder Caddis.

16

Flashback Caddis Larva

Tapered, segmented body • Hare's ear dubbing loop • Varnishing tip

This is a generic pattern for a free-living caddis larva, or one that has vacated its house. For this pattern we use the three most recognisable features: the hard head; the soft fleshy segmented body; the gill-covered body.

Free-living caddis larvae are bottom-dwellers, living amongst the gravel and stones of free-flowing rivers. Extra weight will be needed on most patterns when imitating these, depending on how deep you intend to fish them.

These vulnerable larvae are large, up to 20mm long. They normally anchor themselves to stones with a fine silk thread in order to reduce the possibility of being washed away downstream. But when they are taken by the current, they are a very important trout and grayling food.

The Larva Lace is an excellent material to mimic the soft, fleshy bodies of caddis fly larvae. Some of my favorite colors for this are cream, yellow, green and fluorescent green. Larva Lace is inexpensive and available in several sizes and too many colors to list. So you can customize your Flashbacks, using brighter body colors and glitzy beads, to take advantage of the attractor factor.

This is especially useful when fishing for grayling, who have always been fond of a little extra bling.

The hare dubbing should be a mixture of both hare's ear and hare's mask hair. This comes normally from the European or brown hare. The mask and ears range in color from a pale tan, through a ruddy brown to an almost jet black. The texture and length ranges from fine, woolly under-fur to long, almost bristle-like guard hairs. The ears are covered with very close, fine spiky hair, with almost no underfur.

In this fly we are looking for a blend of both mask and ear hair, to ensure a good range of colors and textures for the traditional dubbing which features in so many patterns.

- **Tapered, segmented body**
  Under- and overbody technique for wrapping a tapered Larva Lace segmented body.

- **Hare's ear dubbing loop**
  Mixing and blending hare's ear and mask hair to create a soft but spiky dubbing that is spun in a dubbing loop and wrapped as a rib.

- **Varnishing bead heads**
  Correct technique for varnishing all bead head patterns so that the head and whip finish are cemented solid.

Tying the Flashback Caddis Larva

THE DRESSING

Hook: Mustad C67S #6-10
Thread: Dyneema
Head: Tungsten bead
Flashback: Pearl tinsel
Body: Flesh colored Larva Lace or nymph rib
Rib: Hare dubbing

WATCH THE VIDEO

youtu.be/s1wOlr8qw-w
Tying the Flashback Caddis Larva
with Barry Ord Clarke

BLENDING HARE'S EAR DUBBING VIDEO

youtu.be/Mxb7IGeEICs
Hare's Ear Dubbing prep part 1
with Barry Ord Clarke

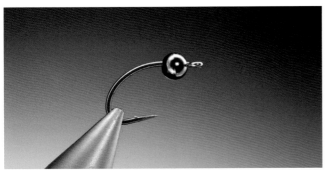

1   Place a heavy tungsten bead onto the hook. Secure your curved caddis hook in the vise, as shown, with the hook shank horizontal.

2   Run a fine foundation of tying thread along top half of the hook shank.

3   For the Flashback you will need some large pearl tinsel.

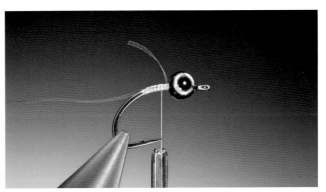

4   Cut a 10cm length of pearl tinsel and tie this in close to the bead head, on top of the hook shank.

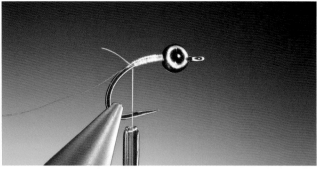

5 Now fold over the tag end, and secure both down the hook shank, into the bend.

6 Cut a 10cm length of Larva Lace and trim the end at a slight angle.

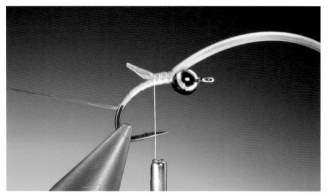

7 Tie in the Larva Lace as shown behind the bead head, with the tapered end towards the rear of the hook.

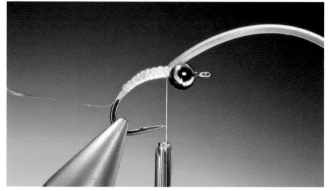

8 Next tie down the Larva Lace with open wraps of tying thread so it forms a slightly tapered segmented body, right up into the bead head.

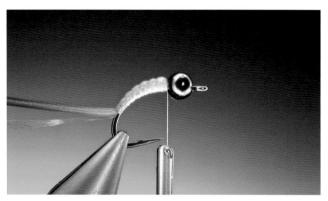

9 Fold over the Larva Lace and repeat the open wraps down into the bend of the hook.

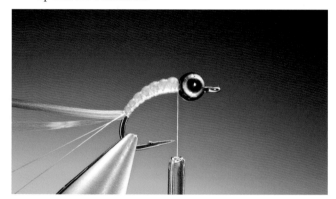

10 Wrap your tying thread down to the tail, make a dubbing loop and wind up again through the segmenting and finish at the bead head.

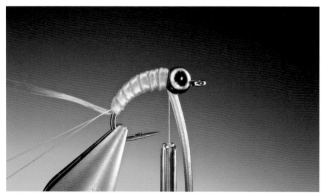

11 Keeping the Flashback tinsel and the dubbing loop at the tail, start by stretching the Larva Lace for the first wrap and then slacken off the tension as you approach the bead head. This will increase the taper on the body. Tie off.

12 Once secure, stretch the Larva Lace again and trim off the excess at the bead head. Wax your dubbing loop and spin a small fine dubbing brush with spiky hare's ear dubbing.

Continued on page 158

13 Fold over the Flashback tinsel and secure with only two loose turns of tying thread. This is important. As you wind the rib, the tinsel will be pulled down between the segmenting.

14 Give the dubbing brush a good brushing to bring out the fibers. You can now carefully wrap your hare's ear dubbing brush rib, making sure that you pull the tinsel down inbetween each segment as you go.

15 Tie off the dubbing brush, trim away the excess tinsel and dubbing loop. Whip finish and remove your tying thread.

16 You should have the Flashback along the upper body, as here. Give the whole body a good brushing, to pull out the spiky dubbing.

17 Re-position the fly in your vise so that it is vertical. Now take a large drop of varnish and place this right in the eye of the hook. The varnish will then disappear down under the bead head. Repeat until it stops draining under the bead. Clean the eye of the hook.

18 The finished Flashback Caddis Larva with a cement solid bead head.

17

Antron Caddis Pupa

Making segmented abdomen • Shuck veiling • Spider-style hackling

This is a nice technique for a realistic segmented caddis pupa body, which demonstrates how, with just a little imagination and ingenuity, a whole new use can be created for a material we have been using for decades.

The adventurous fly tyer is always looking for new materials and solutions to improve fly design. This can be from something they find on the head of a mop, or in an arts and crafts shop, to looking "outside the box" at the use of a traditional material.

When holding flytying tutorials for complete beginners, I always try to emphasize the importance of letting your imagination run wild. Just because a material is generally only used for one technique doesn't mean it has no other applications! Stretch it, melt it, twist it, fold it, burn it . . . The only limit in fly design is your own imagination.

Before you start with the yarn, build up the required taper on the underbody, using your tying thread.

When spinning the yarn, before you start to wrap the caddis pupa body, I recommend that you use a heavy dubbing spinner.

It is critical that the yarn is spun tight and remains tight whilst wrapping. The first few wraps should be made as tight as possible, keeping tension on the spun yarn. But as the wraps approach the mid-section of the body, slacken off a little as you wrap forward towards the thorax. This will emphasize the body taper even more.

The best translucent body effects can be achieved through several thin coats of UV resin. With careful application of the UV resin, you can also determine the final body shape at this stage.

The dubbing for the thorax should be a synthetic long-fibered dubbing which is easy to use and the fibers can be brushed out to form a very convincing larval shuck which veils the Antron body.

The grey partridge is sometimes also called the English or Hungarian partridge. Partridges have declined in Britain, adversely affected by changes in agricultural practice. But whole skins are still available in limited numbers and are by far the most economical. The brown speckled partridge hackle should be one with distinct markings.

If you have a partridge skin, these feathers can be found on the back of the bird. The smallest hackles are found just under the back of the neck, and they increase in size as you go down the back towards the tail.

Once the hackle is selected, grip the tip with one hand and draw the fibers at a 90 degree angle to the stem. Remove any downy fibers and the fibers from the left side, as shown in step 15. Now you have approximately 1cm of fibers remaining on the right side. This will give you the correct amount of hackle.

Once the hackle is wrapped and tied off, it will have the appearance of a classic wet fly spider hackle. Now wet your fingers and stroke the hackle back over the caddis body, enough to hold the hackle fibers in place.

TECHNIQUES MASTERED

- **Segmented abdomen**
  Making a semi-realistic, transparent, segmented pupa body from twisted Antron that is coated with UV resin.

- **Shuck veiling**
  Simple technique for creating a fine dubbing shuck veiling, that can be used not only on pupae but also larvae and nymphs.

- **Perfect partridge hackle**
  How to prepare, position and wrap— spider-style—a speckled partridge hackle with help of a plastic tube.

Then place a small clear plastic tube over the head of the fly so it holds the hackle in position. Put to one side, in a warm place and let it dry. When dry, remove the tube and the fly should be perfect.

Although the natural choice of color for this caddis larva body is a cream or light yellow Antron yarn, try other attractor colors. Antron yarn is inexpensive and available in a wide range of colors. Don't restrict yourself to just Antron, try other yarns and flosses, try the same body technique, but try twisting two different colors or even two different materials together.

Tying the Antron Caddis Pupa

THE DRESSING

Hook: Mustad C49S #10-16
Thread: Cream or tan
Body: Cream Antron yarn and UV resin
Thorax: Very fine creamy yellow
and brown dubbing
Hackle: Speckled partridge hackle

WATCH THE VIDEO

youtu.be/uxVCLf7vuy8
Tying the Antron Caddis Pupa with
Barry Ord Clarke

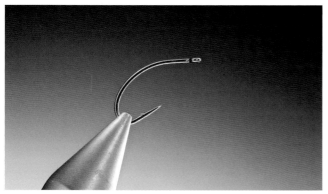

1 Secure your curved caddis hook in the vise, as shown, with the hook shank horizontal.

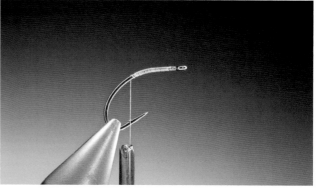

2 Run a fine foundation of tying thread along two-thirds of the hook shank.

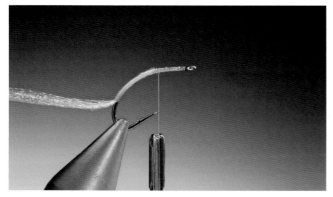

3 Cut a 10cm length of Antron yarn. Tie this in as shown, down into the bend, and run your tying thread up again towards the thorax.

4 Now fold over the other end of the Antron yarn and secure with a couple of loose turns of tying thread. Pull the yarn gently back until almost under the two turns of tying thread.

5 Tie down the Antron on top of the first so that they form a loop. Run your tying thread back up behind the hook eye.

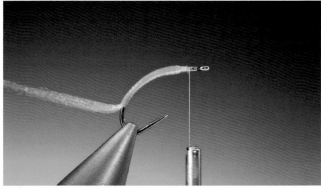

6 Using only wraps of tying thread, build up a slight taper on the body.

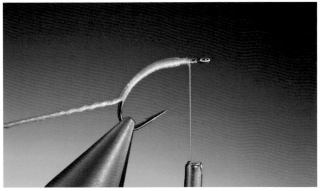

7 You will now need a heavy dubbing spinner. Place the dubbing spinner on the Antron loop and spin tightly.

8 Keeping tension on the dubbing spinner at all times, begin wrapping the Antron noodle all the way up to the thorax in tight, even turns. Tie off with a few tight wraps of tying thread at the thorax.

9 Trim off the excess Antron and secure the ends well, with tying thread.

10 Cover the whole segmented Antron body with a coat of UV resin.

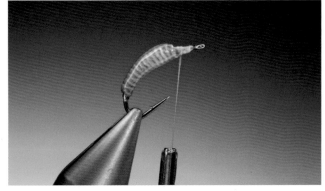

11 Using more coats of UV resin, build up the correct body shape.

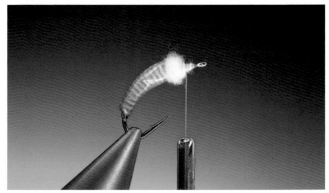

12 Using a long-fibered cream synthetic dubbing, dub half the thorax.

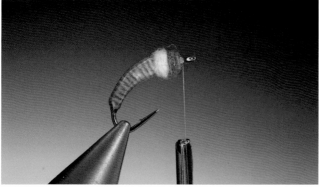

13 Dub the remaining half of the thorax with a brown dubbing of similar style.

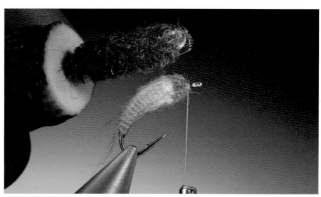

14 With a dubbing brush, pull out the long fibers of the thorax dubbing back over the body as shown. When wet this will represent the gas-filled shuck of the caddis pupa.

15 Select and prepare a speckled partridge hackle, by stripping off one side of the fibers.

16 Tie in the partridge hackle as shown, wound spider-style.

17 Wind on the half hackle so all the fibers are convex. Tie off.

18 Trim off the excess hackle stem. Whip finish, remove your tying thread and varnish.

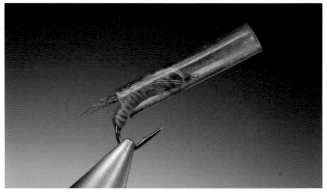

19 Wet the hackle and stroke all the fibers back. Take a clear plastic tube and place over the head of the fly to hold the hackle in place. Remove from the vise and put to one side, to dry.

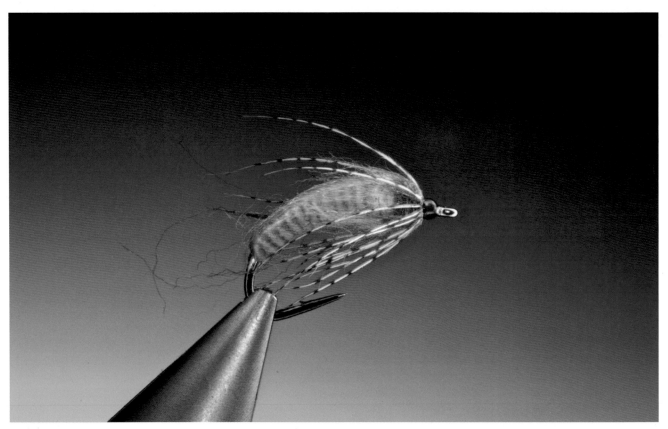

20 When dry, carefully remove the tube, by twisting and pulling at the same time and your fly should be perfect.

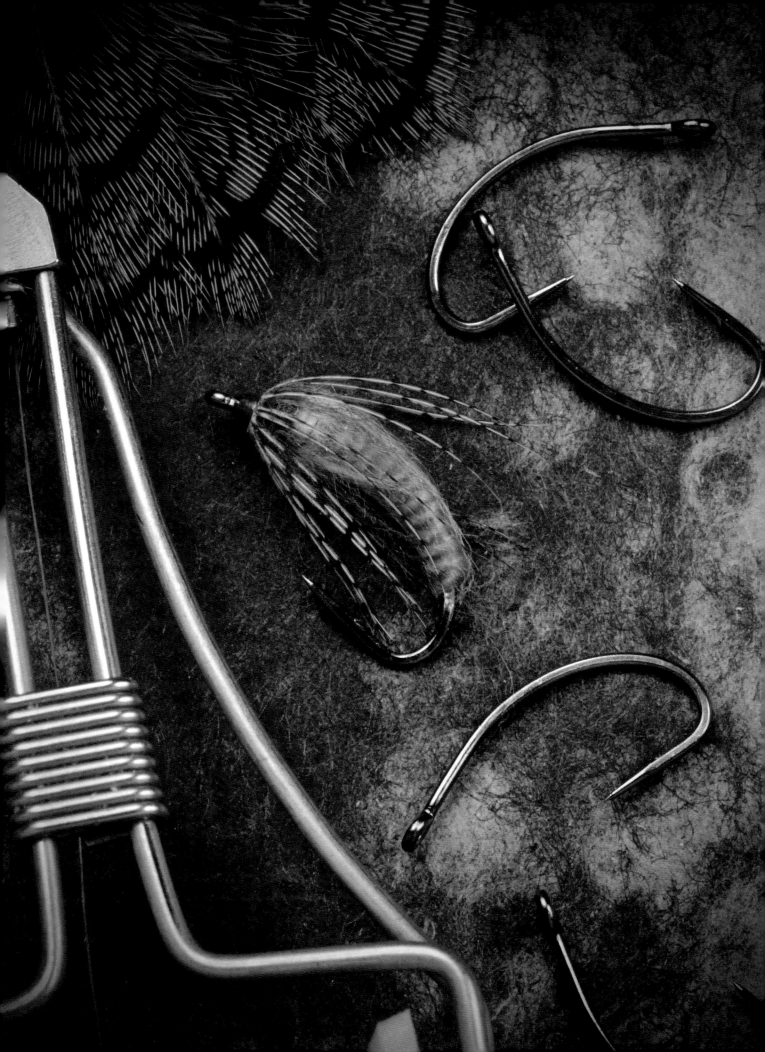

18

G&H Sedge

Deer hair prepping • Deer hair in the dubbing loop • Collar hackling

This technique is an alternative to spinning deer hair flies that don't require a tightly-packed and clipped deer hair body. These 'looser' packed bodies give a more consistent muddler effect, causing more disturbance in the water than the slick, tightly-packed bodies.

For both techniques the best deer hair comes from the winter coat of a northern deer. This hair is more buoyant, filled with small air cells that also cause the hair to flare when put under pressure from the tying thread.

When spinning deer hair in a dubbing loop there are three things that will help: strong tying thread; a good flytying wax; and a heavy dubbing spinner. You can of course manage without these, but they

will improve your deer hair dubbing brush and make your finished fly more robust.

The only tying thread I use for tying with deer hair is Dyneema (*see page 25*) If you can't source Dyneema, you can also use GSP thread. Both these threads enable you to spin your deer hair dubbing brush as tightly as possible, flaring the deer hair evenly at 90 degrees from the core of the brush. This is important if you wish to achieve fine, even clipped bodies.

Deer hair from a winter coat is coarse and thick and a heavy dubbing spinner will put the thread under maximum pressure without breaking when spun into a dubbing brush.

If you know a hunter and are able to get your hands on a skin from European roe deer shot during the winter months, this is excellent hair for spinning.

The skin is not difficult to prepare at home: all you need is a little salt and an hour of your time, scraping away any remaining fat and flesh from the hide, then somewhere dry and airy to nail it up to dry.

The advantage with preparing a skin yourself is not just a financial one. Practically all the deer hair patches that you buy have been processed, washed and tanned. This removes all the fats and oils that the hair is naturally coated in.

On the other hand, natural hair that has not been processed has a waxy, powdery feel to it. This is the deer's natural secretion of what is thought to be keratin, to waterproof the hair, similar to that of a bird and preening oils. This not only improves buoyancy but also increases tying thread purchase when used.

TECHNIQUES MASTERED

- **Deer hair prep**
  How to select and prepare deer hair in a Magic Tool to create spun and clipped deer hair bodies.

- **Deer hair dubbing loop**
  Learn the technique for spinning a deer hair dubbing brush. The method for creating a tapered, clipped deer hair body.

- **Collar hackle**
  A different style of hackle preparation and wrapping of a traditional dry fly collar hackle.

Below: To cut neat strips from deer hair patches I use a furrier's knife. This is a special tool used in the fur industry, designed for cutting furs and leather. The knife has a diagonal blade holder, which accepts extremely sharp razor blades that makes it an ideal tool for precise cutting of not only hair and fur patches but also capes.

Tying the G&H Sedge

THE DRESSING

Hook: Mustad R43 #6-14
Thread: Dyneema
Body: Deer hair winter coat
or spinning hair
Hackle: Red brown saddle hackle

WATCH THE VIDEO

youtu.be/oXjViyzie-U
Tying a G&H Sedge with
Barry Ord Clarke

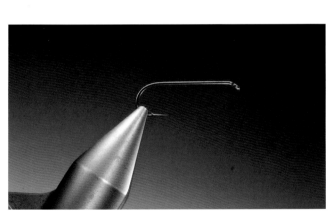

1   Secure your dry fly hook in the vise, as shown, with the hook shank horizontal.

2   Run a fine foundation of tying thread along two-thirds of the hook shank.

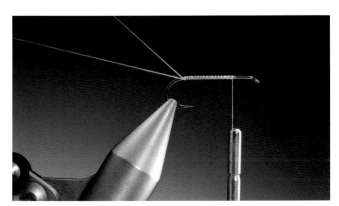

3   Make a dubbing loop with your tying thread at the rear of the hook. Make sure that the two ends of the loop closest to the hook shank are tight together. Run your tying thread forward as shown.

4   Because deer hair is a coarse material, you will need a heavy dubbing spinner to apply sufficient pressure in order to make the hair flare.

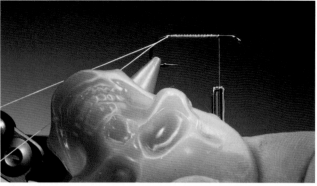

5 If you are using Dyneema tying thread, apply a little wax to the dubbing loop. This will give more purchase between the thread and the hair.

6 Cut a strip of deer hair about the width of a regular deer hair patch. You can also attach your clip direct to a deer hair patch.

7 Using a pair of long straight scissors, trim off the tips of the hair at an angle, as shown.

8 Place the strip in a Magic Clip.

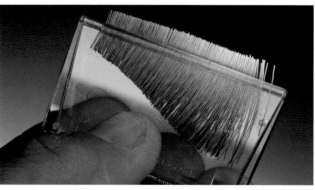

9 Using the long straight scissors again, cut away the hide strip.

10 Now place the deer hair in the dubbing loop, with the longest hair closest to the hook shank. Remember to retain tension on the loop at all times.

11 Attach your dubbing spinner and spin anti-clockwise, until the hair flares evenly and forms a dubbing brush which resembles a miniature Christmas tree.

12 Once the dubbing brush has spun evenly you can begin to wrap it in tight, even turns, from bend to eye.

13 When you have wrapped the whole brush, tie it off. Make sure that you have enough space between the deer hair and the hook eye for your hackle.

14 Make a whip finish and trim off the remaining end of the dubbing loop. Give the deer hair body a good brushing with a toothbrush, which will release any trapped hairs.

15 Now you can make four or five cuts, from the rear of the hook around the whole body.

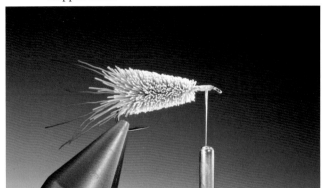

16 Your spun deer hair body should now be round and gently tapered towards the eye end of the hook.

17 Trim off the long hairs at the rear of the body.

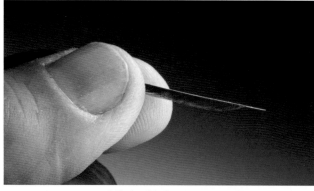

18 Prepare a saddle hackle by stripping off 5mm of the fibers from one side and 50mm of the fibers from the other.

19 Tie in your hackle tight into the deer hair body, so it stands 90 degrees from the hook shank.

20 Attach your hackle pliers and wrap the hackle, so that with each turn, the hackle stem sits tight into the last. Tie off.

21 Cut away the remaining surplus hackle and whip finish.

Sedge Hog Variant

Stacking deer hair • Spinning, trimming, and singeing deer hair

The original sedge hog pattern came from the tying bench of Orkney angler Sandy Nicholson, and was designed as a semi-buoyant wet fly for stillwater trout.

In this adaptation I have excluded the seal's fur body and the front hackle, as per the original, and I use only deer hair to represent the larger members of the caddis family. It works not only on my home brown trout waters here in Norway, but it has also proven to be a deadly attractor pattern fished as a surface lure, when night fishing for sea trout.

The large wing and tightly-packed and trimmed deer hair body render this pattern almost un-sinkable, but when tying this style of deer hair wing, attention should be given to preparing each bunch of hair correctly before tying them in.

Start by cutting a bunch that is a little larger than the one you need because it will reduce significantly when cleaned. Hold the bunch in one hand by the tips. Using a comb, remove all the underfur and the shorter hairs. This is very important when spinning deer hair, as the underfur will act as an anchor and restrict the spinning process.

The shorter hairs will create a somewhat uneven wing when stacking in a hair stacker, so if you want optimal results, you must be very precise in removing as much as possible of both. If necessary, stack the hair after the first cleaning and repeat, with each bunch.

The rear, or first bunch for the tail, need not to be stacked, but should be tied in as a flared spinning

175   THE FEATHER BENDER

bunch, so the tips are evenly distributed around the rear of the hook shank.

The next two or three bunches, depending on what size hook you are using, have to be tied in a little differently. These should be stacked on top of the previous bunch, keeping the tips on top of the hook shank, but still spinning the butt ends of the hair, on the underside of the hook shank.

This is done by first spinning your bobbin anti-clockwise, to give the tying thread a flat profile. Doing this reduces the possibility of cutting the deer hair when pressure is applied through the bobbin.

Then, make two loose wraps of tying thread around the hair bunch before tightening by pulling downwards on your bobbin. This will flare the hair 90 degrees from the hook shank.

Before you release pressure on the bobbin after tightening, make a few zigzag wraps forward through the butt ends and finish with five or six tight turns of thread in front of the bunch to lock it off, ready for the next bunch. This will stop the wing from slipping around the hook shank.

If you wish to obtain optimal buoyancy with this pattern it is important that you use deer hair from a good dense winter coat; this is normally marketed as all-round spinning hair.

TECHNIQUES MASTERED

- **Stacking**
  How to select and prepare the correct amount of deer hair and tie in as a semi-raised wing with flared spun deer hair belly.

- **Spinning**
  Technique for tying a tightly spun and packed deer hair belly with only the butt ends of deer hair.

- **Trimming and singeing of deer hair**
  Special technique for finishing spun and packed deer hair to get a super-tight and smooth finish to the trimmed surface.

But if, like me, you are lucky enough to hunt, or know a hunter, you will have the opportunity of harvesting some of the best roe deer spinning hair possible. The densest hair comes from the center back, also called the saddle. From a roe deer which has lived in the northern hemisphere, this hair can be 6 to 7cm thick.

Tying the Sedge Hog Variant

THE DRESSING

Hook: Mustad R30 #8-14
Thread: Dyneema or GSP
Body: Natural deer hair—winter coat
Wing: Natural deer hair—winter coat

WATCH THE VIDEO

youtu.be/XTui8mSezKs

Tying the Sedge Hog Variant with Barry Ord Clarke

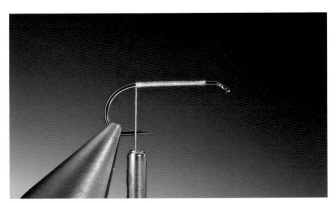

1 Secure your dry fly hook in the vise, as shown, with the hook shank horizontal. Run a fine foundation of tying thread along the hook shank.

2 If you intend to tie a few of these, I find it more efficient to cut 1cm strips of deer hair hide. A 1cm x 10cm strip is enough hair for three size 8 and 10 flies.

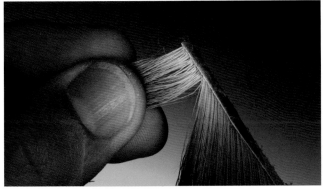

3 Once you have cut your strip, grasp a large bunch of hair at the bottom of the strip.

4 Keeping hold of the bunch, cut it away from the hide.

5 Tie in this first bunch at the rear of the hook as shown and described earlier.

6 Carefully trim away the flared butt ends in front of the wing, on top of the hook shank.

7 Now cut a second bunch of hair and tie this in as the first, but a little longer. Keep hold of the hair tips only, on top of the hook shank, so they don't spin around the hook when flared.

8 Trim off the butt ends, as in step 6.

9 The remaining bunch should be cleaned and stacked in a hair stacker, before tying in.

10 Tie this in, keeping hold of the hair tips only, on top of the hook shank, so they don't spin around the hook when flared. Tie in right behind the hook eye.

11 Whip finish and remove your tying thread.

12 Using a dubbing brush or an old toothbrush, give the fly a good brushing to free any hairs that may be trapped. This will make for a much better finish when clipped.

13 Turn your vise, or fly if you don't have a true rotary vise, upside down. With one straight cut, trim away the deer hair on the underside of the hook.

14 Now carefully cut away any remaining butt ends of hair on the side of the fly as shown. This is best done with serrated scissors.

15 You can now form the muddler-style head by trimming around the hook eye.

16 Using a lighter set at a low flame, carefully singe, but don't burn away, the trimmed ends of the deer hair.

17 Once done, you can use the edge of your scissors to scrape away the soot.

18 View from below. It makes a huge difference, when fished, if the body is formed as a keel on a boat. This will make the fly fish high in the surface and gurgle when pulled.

19 The finished sedge hog variant with a sculpted body and head.

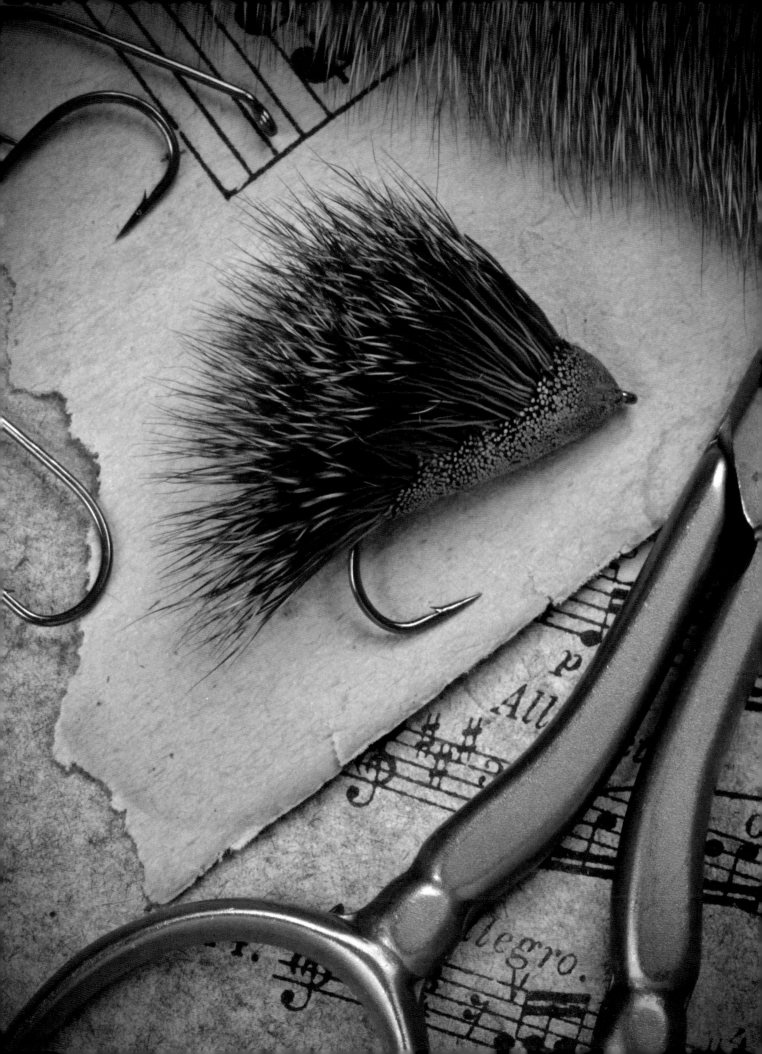

Variegated Sedge Hog

....
THE DRESSING
....

Hook: Mustad R30 #8-14
Thread: Dyneema or GSP
Body: Mixed colored spinning deer hair
Wing: Mixed colored spinning deer hair

VARIANT

After struggling for many years to mix deer hair efficiently, here is a simple method I developed to mix different colors of hair and buck tail.

In order to achieve a good even mix, you will first need a rectangular plastic hook box.

You then have to determine how much deer hair you require for the pattern to be tied. The hair should be a little shorter than the box being used, which ensures that the hairs stay parallel with each other and the tips in the same direction.

If you need three bunches of natural hair for the original pattern, select the three colors you would like to mix and cut and clean each of the bunches, to give you three bunches of evenly-mixed multicolored deer hair.

When cleaning the hair you must be meticulous. If you fail to remove ALL the underfur and shorter hairs, the hair will not mix evenly.

Although a little time-consuming, this is a useful exercise in proportions and in material preparation, and if applied throughout your flytying generally, it will result in better flies, faster.

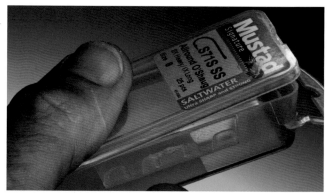

1 Take an elongated plastic hook box or similar one with a clasp lock top makes the process easier.

2 Cut and clean the first bunch of deer hair. Make sure that all the underfur and shorter hair is removed. The hair should be a little shorter than the length of the box, which ensures that the hair stays parallel, with the tips in the same direction.

3 Choose your remaining colors of deer hair and place with the first lot.

4 You will now need two nails that are the same length as the hair to be mixed.

5 Place the two nails in the box with the hair and close the lid. Shake the box from side to side so the nails rattle around.

6 After a few seconds of shaking you should see the hair has been mixed nicely. You can also 'stack' your hair in the box by tapping it vertically on the table, as you would with a regular hair stacker.

7 Use the hair as you would with the sedge hog variant.

20

Para-weld Caddis

Mallard breast wing • CDC twist and wrap • Para-weld cock hackle

The beautifully-marked hen mallard breast feathers used in this pattern can create realistic caddis wings if prepared and used correctly. This little-used material is generally sold in small packets of loose feathers, of which you will most likely find that many are, unfortunately, unusable. I like to dispose of all the poor quality feathers and sort all the remaining ones before I start tying with them.

I do this by emptying the whole packet into a clear plastic box. Start by picking out any feathers that are too fluffy, have bent or twisted stems or are just downright ugly.

Then I strip away the downy material from the base of every remaining feather and sort them into size. This makes tying with them not only quicker when selecting but also more pleasurable.

Once you have selected your two breast feathers of a similar size, check that you have stripped away all the downy material at the base of the feather stem on both feathers.

Now carefully pull away some more fibers from each side of the feathers to leave a neat caddis-wing shape (*see Step 10*).

Once you are happy with the shape and size of both your mallard breast feathers, place them, concave side up, on top of each other. At this stage don't trim off the stems—you will need these soon.

Place both wings on top of the caddis body and secure at the thorax, with only a couple of loose turns of tying thread. If the wraps of tying thread here are too tight, the wing will not sit correctly.

Now take hold of the breast feather stems, both at once, and gently pull into position. You can also maneuver the wings, by moving them a little from side to side. Once you are happy with the wing length and location, secure with tighter wraps of tying thread.

The polypropylene used for the post in this technique requires a test before use. I found several of the polypropylene yarns I tried under development, troublesome. They burned, wouldn't melt at a low temperature, or lost their color when melted. So just do a little heat test with the different polypropylene yarns you have to hand, before you start.

The color of the polypropylene yarn used is entirely up to you. You can make it discreet, matching the color of the wing or the body of the pattern being tied, or as vibrant and visible as possible, doubling as a quick sight indicator, for low light conditions or on broken water.

For the post you will need a 10cm length of polypropylene yarn. This can be attached by using the lift and lower technique. Holding the poly yarn by both ends, fold the yarn in two, around your hanging tying thread. Take hold of both ends at the rear of the vise in one hand and lift your tying thread, then lower the tying thread. Your poly yarn should now be trapped in position, on top of the hook shank.

- **Mallard breast wing**
  Feather preparation and technique for a realistic caddis-style roof wing made with two hen mallard breast feathers.

- **CDC twist and wrap**
  Technique for using a CDC hackle to create a very buoyant and slender CDC segmented body.

- **Para-weld cock hackle**
  How to prepare and wrap a parachute hackle with a traditional cock hackle for use with the Para-weld technique.

When you come to melt the para post, and weld your hackle in place, it's best to use a cautery pen. These are inexpensive and very useful to have on your tying bench. If you don't have one, and you are careful, you can also use a lighter, but take care you don't burn your hackle, or set the whole fly on fire.

Left: A cautery pen is not only useful for precisely melting the post on your para-weld hackles but it is a great tool to have lying around on your tying bench. If you are tying patterns such as Intruders or Snakes, it makes easy work of cutting Superbraid lines. It's also perfect for removing single stray fibers and hairs, or even clearing unwanted material from a hook eye.

Tying the Para-weld Caddis

WATCH THE VIDEO

youtu.be/3PU4vY2g-cI
Tying the Para-weld Caddis with
Barry Ord Clarke

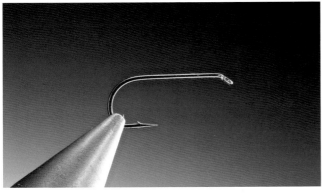

1 Secure your dry fly hook in the vise, as shown, with the hook shank horizontal.

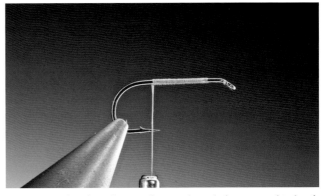

2 Run a fine foundation of tying thread along two-thirds of the hook shank.

3 Select a CDC hackle with long fibers in a color of your choice.

4 With only two loose turns of tying thread, attach the CDC hackle to the hook shank. Carefully pull the CDC hackle through the turns of tying thread, until the tip fibers are shorter than the hook shank.

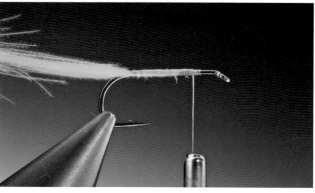

5 Now wrap the tying thread forward over the CDC and finish a little behind the hook eye.

6 Attach a hackle plier to the end of the CDC hackle. Twist the CDC hackle as you wrap forward and form the segmented body.

7 When you reach the tying thread, tie off the CDC and trim away the excess stem.

8 Using straight sharp scissors, trim off any CDC fibers from the body.

9 Select two hen mallard breast feathers. Look for two with good markings, level tips and of similar size.

10 Strip away the downy fibers and the lower part of both the feathers.

11 Make sure they are the same size, and correct wing size for the hook you are using.

12 Place both the hackles on top of each other and secure with a couple of loose turns of tying thread.

13 You can position the wing by taking hold of both the stems, then carefully adjust them into position.

14 Once you are happy with the wing, secure with a few firm turns of tying thread.

15 The wing from above should look like a upside-down canoe.

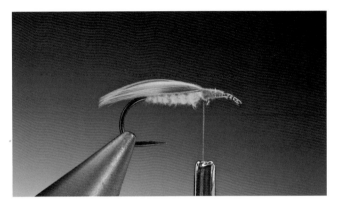

16 Trim away the excess mallard feather and finish with a few wraps of tying thread.

17 Apply a little dubbing to the tying thread and make two or three turns at the rear of the thorax.

18 Tie in a length of poly yarn for the parachute post.

19 Wrap the base of the post with tying thread. Place a small drop of head cement on the post base.

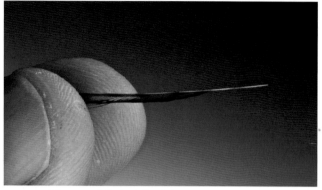

20 Select a saddle hackle of the correct size and strip away the fibers from the stem base and along the entire length of one side.

21 Tie in your hackle at the post base with only a couple of turns of tying thread. Now take hold of the hackle stem and pull down until the hackle is correctly placed.

22 Trim off, and tie down the remaining hackle stem.

23 Dub the remaining thorax, whip finish.

24 Remove the tying thread and place the hook vertically in the vise.

25 Re-attach your tying thread on the post and wrap down tight into the thorax.

Continued page 192

26 Attach a hackle plier to the hackle and wrap in tight neat turns in towards the thorax. Make sure that each turn is positioned tight in to the last.

27 Trim the post down to about 1cm long. Tie off the hackle.

28 Remove the excess hackle. Whip finish in-between the hackle and thorax.

29 Return the hook to the original position in the vise. Remove the tying thread.

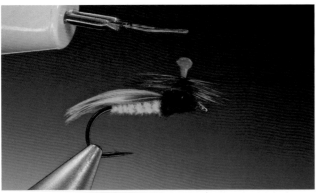

30 Now take a cautery tool and carefully melt the poly post gradually down into the hackle. Take your time with this and try not to burn it.

31 Once melted correctly, the poly yarn will weld the hackle in place and form a neat even bead, on top of the hackle center.

32 The para-weld caddis as seen from above.

33 As seen from below.

21

Golden Olive Streaking Caddis

Preparing, stacking, and winging with deer hair

The Streaking Caddis has truly established its status as a modern classic, since it was created by Swedish flytying guru, Lennart Bergqvist. Without a doubt it is the most popular caddis fly pattern in Scandinavia. Originally tied with natural deer hair on a size 8 hook to imitate the huge adult *Phryganea grandis* caddis fly, it is now tied on a variety of hook sizes, not only for trout fishing, but also as a surface lure for salmon and sea trout.

Over the past thirty years or more I believe that it is this pattern that I have been asked most often to demonstrate and teach other tyers to make.

Although the Streaking Caddis appears to be a simple pattern to tie, it does present us with a couple of challenging techniques. The most common

mistake when tying this pattern is to use more than one bunch of deer hair for the wing and head.

One of the most fundamental factors for success when tying with deer hair is preparation. Over the years I have become so meticulous, when it comes to this, that I'm sure I would rate as a severe case on the OCD scale. Each bunch of deer hair should be cleaned before you use it. Removing the underfur and shorter hairs is a very important part of this ritual. To do this correctly it helps to have a few tools, a good hair comb, a toothbrush and a heavy hair stacker.

I hope I have persuaded you to take a little time preparing the bunch of deer hair, before you tie it in. Start by cutting a bunch that is considerably

larger than the one you'll need. It will reduce in size significantly when cleaned.

Hold the bunch in one hand by the tips. Now, using a comb, remove all the underfur and the shorter hairs. You may have to repeat this procedure to remove it all. This is very important when spinning deer hair, as the underfur will act as an anchor and restrict the spinning process.

The shorter hairs will create a somewhat uneven wing when stacking in a hair stacker, so if you want optimal results, you must be very precise in removing as much as possible of both short hairs and underfur.

If necessary, stack the hair after the first cleaning and repeat.

TECHNIQUES MASTERED

- **Cleaning deer hair**
  Cleaning, prepping and stacking of a deer hair bunch for an all-in-one combined down wing and muddler head.

- **Deer hair down wing**
  Tying technique for securing a single bunch of deer hair for an adult caddis-style down wing.

- **Muddler-style head**
  How to prepare, correctly trim and singe spun deer hair for a perfect muddler-style head finish.

Golden Olive Streaking Caddis

THE DRESSING

Hook: Mustad R30 #8-16
Thread: Dyneema or GSP
Body: Super-fine dubbing
Wing: Golden olive dyed spinning
deer hair

WATCH THE VIDEO

youtu.be/AWxGo2d8EnY
Tying the Golden Olive Streaking Caddis
with Barry Ord Clarke

1 Secure your dry fly hook in the vise, as shown, with the hook shank horizontal. Run a fine foundation of tying thread along the hook shank.

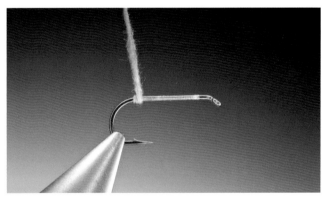

2 The body for the Streaking Caddis should be dubbed nice and tight with a good synthetic dry fly dubbing. Start your dubbing off at the rear of the hook. Once you've caught it in to the hook shank, spin it tighter onto the thread.

3 Increase the amount of dubbing as you wrap forward so you get a gradual cigar taper, about two-thirds of the way along the hook shank, keeping it tight all the way.

4 Cut a large bunch of deer hair and grip it in one hand by the tips.

5 Comb out all the underfur and shorter hairs from the bunch.

6 Place the bunch in a medium hair stacker. The hair should fill the stacker but not be so tight that it makes it difficult to remove.

7 Make sure that your tying thread is positioned tight into the dubbed abdomen and that you have spun your bobbin anti-clockwise so that it attains a flat profile.

8 Stack the cleaned deer hair in a stacker and measure the wing along the body of the fly.

9 While holding the hair in your left hand on top of the hook shank, make the first turn of tying thread around only the hair, not the hook shank, and then two loose turns around both the hair and hook shank.

10 Retaining the wing in your left hand, zig-zag the tying thread forward along the deer hair to the hook eye. Whip finish and remove your tying thread. Use a toothbrush to brush out any trapped deer hair.

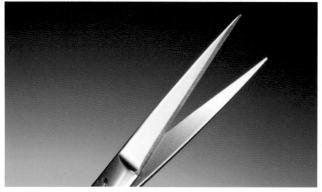

11 If you have serrated scissors, use them to trim the head of the fly.

12 Rotate your vise and make the first cut horizontal on the underside of the hook shank.

13 Now make a few more cuts at an angle around the head, taking care not to cut the wing.

14 Trim the head until a basic bullet-head shape is formed.

15 Grasp the wing tightly with your left hand to protect it from the flame. Take your lighter on a medium flame setting and carefully singe around the whole clipped head of the fly, taking care not to burn it, or even worse, set fire to it!

16 Once you have singed the head, take the edge of your scissors and brush off the soot.

17 You should now have a super-fine, smooth muddler-type head that follows the angle of the wing.

22

The Mutant

Using Melt Glue • Realistic ant bodies • Hackle tip wings

Tying with melt glue does require a little more practice and patience than most regular materials, but perseverance is the key here. I apologize for the pun, but "stick with it." Melt glue is a material that one has to get used to. Once mastered, it can be put to use not only in developing new patterns but also as a substitute for existing materials.

Using a proper rotary vise makes tying with melt glue a whole lot easier.

Melt glue or Hot Melt Adhesive (HMA) is a form of thermoplastic adhesive that is used in a heat gun, commonly supplied in cylindrical sticks in various sizes, from hobby to industrial. I find the hobby size not only the cheapest but also the easiest to apply. Another advantage with the hobby gun is the amount of different glue that is available.

Although for this pattern I use a colored glue, in many patterns I use the transparent or "regular"

glue that can also be colored with waterproof felt markers. The regular glue is also much easier to handle and shape than the colored. In most cases, it has a lower melting temperature and a shorter drying time than the glues with added color and glitter. Most melt glue pistols and glues have a heat "melting" temperature printed on the packet.

After tying with melt glue for nearly two decades, nowadays I seldom use my gun to apply the glue, only for patterns where a large amount of glue is required.

If you are applying glue to the hook with the gun, you may find finishing a little difficult. When you have applied the amount required and try to remove the gun, the glue from the hook to the gun nozzle will stretch like a spider's web.

You can eliminate this problem by taking your finger off the trigger of the gun and wrapping the spider web around the hook shank quickly until it releases.

Otherwise I melt the glue direct from the "glue stick" with a lighter, or I first cut the required amount of glue from the stick with scissors or a blade, hold one end of the glue fragment with needle nose tweezers and warm the other end with the lighter and apply it to the hook. I then continue to melt and form the glue with the lighter on the hook.

If your melt glue body is dry, but isn't perfect, you can trim it down to shape with scissors and then warm it again to even up the surface. This can be done as many times as required. The clear glue can be colored by applying a foundation of colored tying thread over the hook shank before you apply the glue.

On a storage note: if you have a tendency to dry your flies and fly boxes over a heater after a trip, I recommend you remove your melt glue patterns first!

On the warmest summer days, the temperature rises in the south-facing ant hills and triggers the annual swarming. Ants are not good flyers, so they leave the nest in large numbers to increase the chances of establishing a new colony. When they take to the

TECHNIQUES MASTERED

- **Using melt glue**
  Introduction to using this extremely useful material for flytying.

- **Realistic ant bodies**
  How to prepare, melt and manipulate the melt glue with use of a full-rotary vise to form perfect little ant bodies.

- **Hackle tip wings**
  Hackle preparation and technique for tying small flat-lying semi-realistic flying ant wings.

wing, they are at the mercy of the wind and end up where it takes them.

If they are unlucky and land on water, the fish go into a feeding frenzy during which I have witnessed the trout taking just about any fly that is presented to them. But other times they can be so selective that they will only take the perfect pattern with the right silhouette, color and behavior. Therefore it is important to have a good imitation, and a more realistic ant imitation than this is difficult to find, without going way over the top and tying an ultra-realistic pattern. This is after all a fishing fly!

Here I have made the two most characteristic body parts with melt glue, that shine just like the natural in the summer sun. This effective pattern is two-colored: one half black, the other half red, which I have found to work when both colors of ant are swarming. Once mastered, the glue part of the pattern takes only one minute to tie!

Undressed, this pattern has an inbuilt drowning effect. As soon as an ant has crash-landed on the water, the rear body part begins to sink, while its legs and wings hold it afloat. If you are going to fish this pattern "high and dry" I recommend that you impregnate it well with float-ant. But it fishes just as well without, as a slow drowner!

Tying the Mutant Melt Glue Ant

THE DRESSING

Hook: Mustad R30 94833 #12-14
Thread: Black
Body: Black and red melt glue
Hackle: Brown saddle hackle

WATCH THE VIDEO

youtu.be/p9T_oeW5enY
Tying the Mutant Melt Glue Ant with
Barry Ord Clarke

1 Melt glue or HMA is versatile material that comes in many colors.

2 Take one black and one red melt glue stick and with a craft knife cut off each about a 5mm slice. You should cut a disc like this.

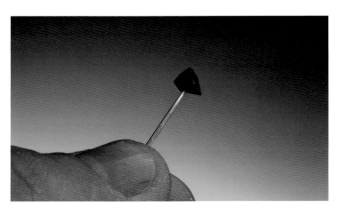

3 Cut the disk in half and then each half into three equal wedges. Cut a smaller piece of red glue for the head.

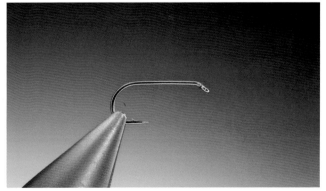

4 Secure your dry fly hook in the vise. Make sure that the hook shaft is horizontal. If you have a true rotary vise, center the hook.

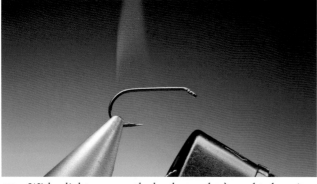

5 With a lighter, warm the hook; you don't need to have it glowing red, just warm enough to melt the glue. About two seconds in the flame will do, any warmer and the glue will run off.

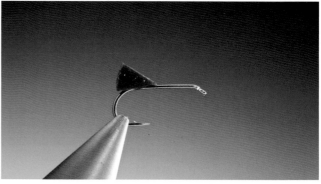

6 While the hook is still warm, take the larger piece of melt glue and press it down onto the warm hook as shown. The glue will set quickly so you don't need to hold it there.

7 Now take your lighter again and warm the glue but don't burn it! As it warms slowly it starts to melt, and it will naturally flow around the hook shank. The warm glue will retain a level of viscosity.

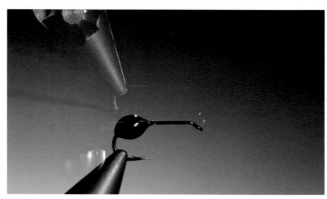

8 Rotate your vise and the hook to get the body nicely distributed around the hook and the perfect shape. Remove your lighter and continue rotating until dry.

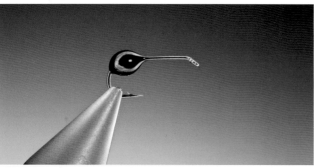

9 Once the glue is dry, which only takes a few seconds, you should have the perfect abdomen.

10 Now take the smaller piece of red melt glue.

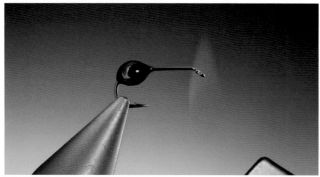

11 Next you warm the front of the hook, but again, not too much. If you warm the front of the hook too much, the heat will travel down the hook shank and the rear body will melt again. So take care!

12 Stick the smaller red glue wedge at the front of the hook.

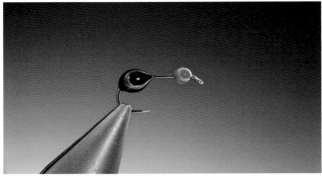

13 Warm again. Rotate and cool. Your ant body is complete. Back to normal tying.

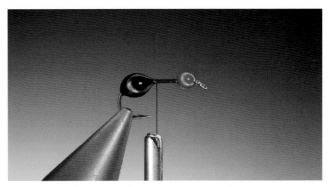

14 Attach your tying thread on the hook shank between the abdomen and head.

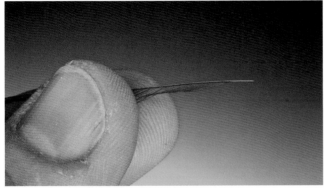

15 Prepare a brown saddle hackle by stripping off the barbs to create a bare strip 5mm on one side and 50mm on the other.

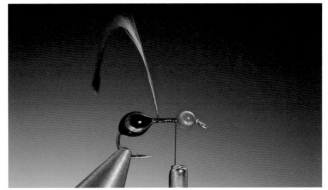

16 Tie in the hackle, tight into the abdomen. Run your tying thread forward towards the head.

17 Wind on the hackle towards the head and tie off. You can make this hackle as dense or as sparse as you like. Whip finish and remove your tying thread. Your finished Mutant is ready to fish.

Carpenter Ant
(Flying Mutant)

VARIANT

THE DRESSING

Hook: Mustad R30 94833 #12-16
Thread: Black
Body: Black melt glue
Wings: Two blue dun hackle tips
Hackle: Black saddle hackle

WATCH THE VIDEO

youtu.be/GKq367ZfPNs

Tying the Carpenter Ant with
Barry Ord Clarke

1 Make your melt glue body as above. For the larger Carpenter ant, an elongated abdomen is required.

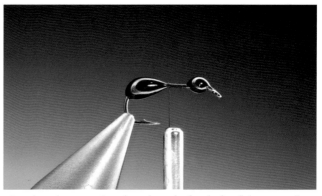

2 Attach your tying thread on the hook shank between the abdomen and head.

3 Select two blue dun hackle tips of the same size and shape for the wings.

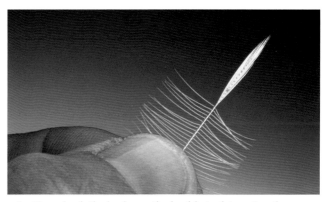

4 Draw back the barbs on the hackle to determine the wing size.

5 Tie in the wings one each side of the abdomen as shown.

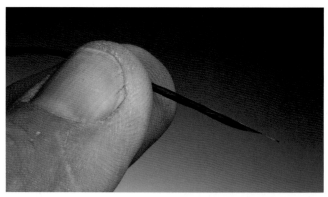

6 Prepare a saddle hackle by stripping off the barbs to create a bare strip 5mm on one side and 50mm on the other.

7 Tie the hackle in at the wing base and run your tying thread forward to the head.

8 Wind on the hackle towards the head and tie off. You can make this hackle as dense or as sparse as you like.

9 Whip finish and remove your tying thread. Now trim away the hackle barbs on the underside of the hook only.

10 The flying carpenter ant as seen by the fish.

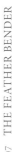

23

Hawthorn Fly

Reverse CDC winging • Knotting legs • Yarn wing casing

The Hawthorn Fly or *bibio marci* as it is also known, is easily recognisable when airborne by its long gangly rear legs that dangle behind it as it flies.

The hatches of this terrestrial are short-lived, very intense, and normally in huge numbers, often swarming over riverbank hedgerows and vegetation in a mating dance. As with flying ants, the hawthorn fly is an inferior aviator and is put to the mercy of the wind when on the wing, carried wherever it blows. If this happens to be to the river, the angler can experience some fast and furious dry fly sport.

The main features of this seasonal delicacy are the black hair body, long legs and large head. Unlike its close relative the black gnat, this is a large fly, which can be up to 12mm long. All these are identifying features and trigger factors to consider when tying.

During mating, the male and female hawthorn fly cling to each other rather awkwardly, while on the wing. This results in an even more blunderingly poor display of flight and on many occasions results in the couple kamikazeing in a love embrace into the river. This brace of flies are often favored by feeding trout over the singles, which they allow to drift by. Size matters!

I am fortunate enough to have shooting for capercaillie (the largest member of the grouse family) on my doorstep, and both the cock and hen of this magnificent bird provide the fly tyer with some striking plumage.

Barbs from the tail feather of the male capercaillie provide us with a long slender herl that can be put to good use on the bodies of not only dry flies, but also as wing cases on nymphs. If you are not as lucky as I am with capercaillie on the doorstep, you can substitute its herl for turkey or even swan herl for the rear legs and body.

The herl from these birds, when wound with precision, creates the most beautiful hairy segmented bodies and it is worth spending some time experimenting with them.

When a natural that I'm trying to imitate has such defining features as the legs on a daddy-long-legs or the fly in question, the Hawthorn Fly, I like to over-emphasize these features by making them a little larger than life. I find that this is often a game-changer when there are incalculable amounts of them on the water. If you would like to see a little technique for knotting the legs, you can watch the video recommended on page 60.

The reverse CDC wing can be a little fiddly, so if you would like to try an easier method, see page 218 where I use the plastic tube technique for the same result.

When it comes to the wing case, head and legs, I use a single strand of polypropylene yarn in black or dark brown.

- **Herl body and legs**
  Tying a slender hairy herl body and large rear knotted legs, using a longer capercaillie, swan or turkey herl.

- **Reverse CDC wing**
  Traditional technique for mounting a reverse hackle wing using a CDC hackle.

- **Poly yarn wing case and legs**
  Constructing the distinctive hawthorn fly wing case, legs and head from a single strand of polypropylene yarn.

Tie the poly yarn tight into the first half of the ostrich herl body and quite wide, spread over both sides of the thorax, so that when it's pulled over and tied down, with only a couple of turns of tying thread behind the hook eye, it becomes narrower, to form a triangle. Now split the poly yarn into three strands: one large over the hook eye and two smaller, one each side. Secure and whip finish. Remove your tying thread and trim them down to the correct length.

Tying the Hawthorn Fly

THE DRESSING

Hook: Mustad R43 #10-12
Thread: Black
Body: Capercaillie, swan, or turkey herl
Wing: CDC hackle
Rear Legs: Capercaillie, swan, or turkey herl
Wing case: Black polypropylene yarn
Thorax: Black ostrich herl
Hackle: Black

WATCH THE VIDEO

youtu.be/JXR6eesvFc0
Tying a Hawthorn Fly with Barry Ord Clarke

KNOTTING LEGS

youtu.be/EDZ6xZ6ogoQ
Tying Knots in Daddy Legs with
Barry Ord Clarke

1 Secure your extra-long dry fly hook in the vise, as shown, with the hook shank horizontal.

2 Run a fine foundation of tying thread along the center of the hook shank.

3 Cut a few strands of capercaillie or turkey herl and tie in, by the tips, at the rear of the hook.

4 Wrap the herl forward. Take care not to twist the herl or you will lose the hairy effect. Tie off at the thorax.

5 Select a long-fibered CDC hackle in blue dun or white for the wing.

6 Tie in the CDC hackle as shown with a couple of loose turns of tying thread at the thorax.

7 Carefully pull the CDC hackle backwards to form the reverse hackle wing. Secure with a few wraps of tying thread.

8 Trim off the surplus ends of the CDC hackle and tidy up with a few turns of tying thread.

9 Take two long capercaillie herls and knot them to form the leg joints. Tie these in as shown, close to the wing, one each side.

10 Trim off the excess herl from the legs.

11 Select a good-quality black ostrich herl and tie in at the wing base.

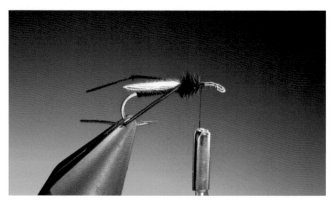

12 Attach a hackle plier and make a few turns of ostrich herl for the hair body section.

13 Cut a short length of polypropylene yarn and tie this in as shown.

14 Tie in another length of black ostrich herl.

15 Prepare a black saddle hackle by stripping off the barbs to create a bare strip 5mm on one side and 50mm on the other.

16 Tie in the hackle and run your tying thread forward, just behind the hook eye.

17 Attach your hackle plier to the ostrich herl and wrap forward to create the hairy thorax. Tie off and remove the excess.

18 Now wind your hackle through the thorax in even, neat turns and secure behind the hook eye.

19 Trim off the hackle fibers on top of the thorax.

20 Take hold of the polypropylene yarn, making sure the fibers are flat, and secure with two or three loose turns of tying thread. Position the poly yarn.

21 Make a couple of turns of tying thread back towards the thorax to secure the poly yarn. Now separate the fibers as shown into two small bunches on each side, then center the remaining bunch over the hook eye. Whip finish.

22 Remove your tying thread. Trim off the poly yarn on the sides to form the legs and the center poly yarn to form the head.

23 The finished Hawthorn Fly.

24

Long-legged Midge

Working with horse hair • Quill body preparation

This little pattern employs a couple of materials that have been somewhat neglected in recent years. Stripped hackle stem was a popular body material in bygone days and many patterns listed this as the body material.

If you are only going to tie a few flies with stripped quill bodies, you can strip them by hand, just by pulling off the barbs, one hackle at a time. But make sure you use quality cock hackle: these have a supple stem that can easily be wrapped without breaking.

If you intend tying a dozen or more, it's worth doing it chemically. Take a glass jar and fill with a 1 to 3 mixture of household bleach and hot water.

Select about a dozen or so hackles, but avoid mixing hackles from different capes or size and thickness as these may vary in burning time.

Place an elastic band around the hackle stems, making a bunch, and hang these in the jar of bleach mixture. After five minutes or so, remove the hackles and rinse in cold water. If there are still any remaining barbs, repeat.

Once stripped, soak for a short while in a jar of clean water mixed with 2 to 3 teaspoons of baking soda, to neutralize the chemical burn. This process can also be used for stripping peacock eye tops, but here the bleaching time should be reduced to between 30 seconds and two minutes only.

Horse hair is another material that has been somewhat forgotten. In the times of Walton and Cotton, horse tail hair was used for making fly lines, leaders and tippets. The hair from a stallion's tail is extremely strong and supple. A single hair could be used to land surprisingly large trout. As a flytying material it was used very effectively for wrapping bodies and, as here, for legs.

The lighter, almost opaque, center tail hairs are easily dyed and can be found on violin bows. These create an almost translucent segmented body effect when wound.

When tying the reverse hackle CDC wing, attention should be paid to the length of barbs on the CDC, so that a nice even wing can be formed.

The wing can be tied without using a plastic tube, but this does make the technique easier, especially if you feel you are all fingers and thumbs when performing intricate procedures.

Tying the Long-legged Midge

THE DRESSING

Hook: Mustad R50 #12-16
Thread: Black
Body: Stripped black cock hackle stem
Legs: Black horse hair
Wing: White or dun cock hackle
Thorax: Black CDC

WATCH THE VIDEO

youtu.be/bqtBH4t9nVk
Tying the Long-legged Midge
with Barry Ord Clarke

1 Secure your dry fly hook in the vise, as shown, with the hook shank horizontal.

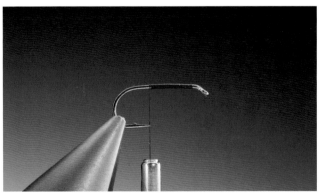

2 Run a fine foundation of tying thread along two-thirds of the hook shank.

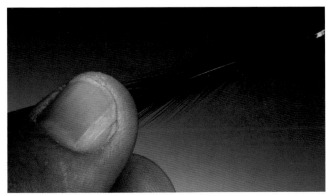

3 Select a long black cock hackle for the body.

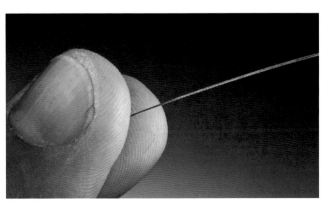

4 Strip off all the barbs from both sides of the black cock hackle.

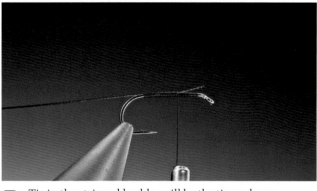

5 Tie in the stripped hackle quill by the tip as shown. This will create an increasingly tapered body towards the thorax.

6 Attach a hackle plier and wrap the stripped hackle quill in tight neat turns, taking care as you go not to twist it. Once wrapped a little over halfway, tie off.

7 Select some black horse hair for the legs.

8 Tie in one length of horse hair to form the rear legs.

9 Wind your tying thread a little forward and tie in the second length of horse hair.

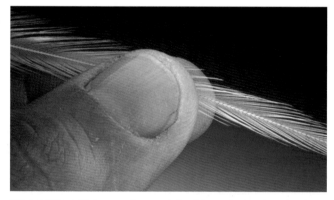

10 Select a white or dun cock hackle with nice long barbs.

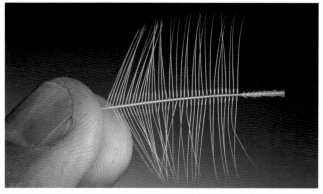

11 Prepare your hackle as shown, taking care that the barbs on each side of the hackle are long enough to make the reverse hackle wing.

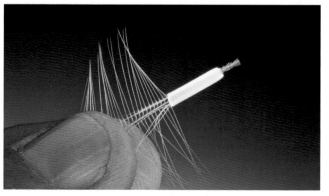

12 Here I use a short length of plastic tube taken from a tube fly. Slide this over the prepared hackle point as shown.

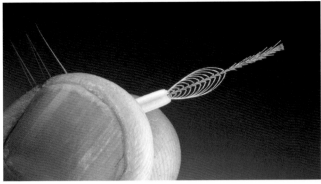

13 Now carefully slide the tube down the hackle to form the correct size of wing required for your hook size.

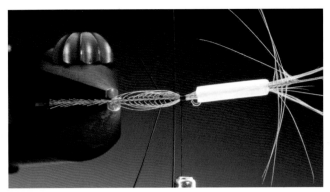

14 Keeping the tube in place on the hackle, secure the wing with a couple of turns of tying thread. This view is from above.

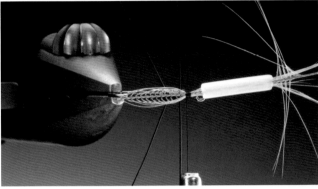

15 Trim off the hackle point as close to the wing as possible without damaging it.

16 Once secure, carefully remove the tube and trim off the excess hackle stem, then anchor the wing with a few more turns of tying thread.

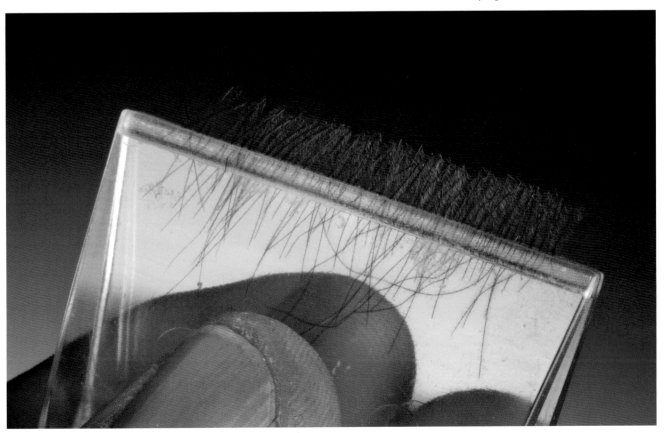

17 Load a black CDC hackle in a Magic Clip, as shown, and cut away the hackle stem.

18 Split your tying thread to form a dubbing loop, place the CDC in the loop and spin, to form a dubbing brush.

19 Wind the CDC forward leaving enough room for the last pair of legs behind the hook eye.

20 Tie in the last remaining legs just behind the hook eye.

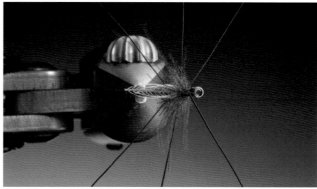

21 Once the legs are in position and secured, whip finish and remove your tying thread.

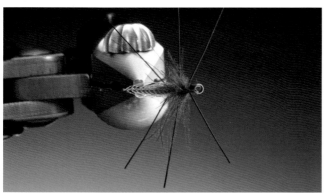

22 Trim the legs down to the correct length.

23 Now using a pair of flat-nosed tweezers, form the joints in the legs as shown by bending the horse hair.

24 The finished Long-legged Midge.

25

Hatching Midge

Quill body-building • Para-welding • Ostrich herl thorax

Another of my para-weld patterns, this one represents a midge pupa at the very last stage immediately before hatching, hanging in the surface film.

Midges are probably the most numerous, and therefore one of the most important, trout foods, in many cases constituting 70 percent of the fish's diet. And it is at the larval and pupal stages that midges are at their most vulnerable.

Unlike the other para-weld mayfly patterns, where I require a tapered abdomen that thickens towards the thorax, the midge's body needs to remain slender throughout. We can achieve this by using another technique for attaching the parachute post to the hook shank, which results in minimal build-up of tying thread.

Most polypropylene yarn is sold wrapped around a card. If you cut one whole wrap of polypropylene from the card, you have a V-shaped length, (*see step 6*) from a standard card, which is approximately 12cm long. This is the perfect working length: minimal waste but yet enough to remain manageable.

While holding the V-shaped piece, one end in each hand with the fold nearest to you, place one end each side of the tying thread.

Then holding both ends of the polypropylene in one hand, lift it vertically, so it lifts the tying thread, on top of the hook shank.

Let it down gently so the weight of your bobbin holds it in place on top of the hook shank. You can now secure the post in position.

The body requires a long barbed tail feather. I am fortunate enough to have capercaillie (largest member of the grouse family) hunting on my doorstep, and both the male and female of this magnificent bird provide the fly tyer with some striking plumage.

You can substitute the capercaillie barb with turkey or even swan in the color of your choice. The barbs from these birds, when wound with precision, create the most beautiful segmented bodies and are worth spending some time experimenting with.

If you want the perfect parachute hackle, a few things must be considered and executed correctly, before you tie in your hackle.

Once you have mounted your post, take a little time in wrapping a good firm base to the post with tying thread. This should be long enough to accompany the thorax and the amount of hackle wraps desired for the particular pattern you are tying.

For the body, if you can't get a capercaillie tail feather (and one is enough for many years' tying) then domestic white turkey tail quills that are dyed and normally sold as condor substitute are an acceptable substitute for capercaillie. They have extremely long barbs and are available in a wide range of colors, both natural and vivid, and make good herl bodies.

- **Creating a herl body**
  Tying a slender hairy herl emerger body, using a longer capercaillie, swan or turkey herl.

- **Para-weld hackle**
  How to prepare and wrap a parachute hackle with a traditional cock hackle using the para-weld technique.

- **Ostrich herl thorax**
  Tying a realistic-behaving black ostrich herl thorax that will pulsate beneath the para-weld hackle in the water.

Tying the Hatching Midge

THE DRESSING

Hook: Mustad C49 #10-20
Thread: Same color as body
Post: Polypropylene yarn
Body: One capercaillie, swan, or turkey herl
Thorax: Black ostrich herl
Hackle: Blue dun

WATCH THE VIDEO

youtu.be/VXA2bFVQHtc

Tying a Hatching Midge
with Barry Ord Clarke

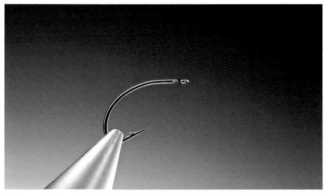

1 Secure your hook in the vise, as shown, with the hook shank horizontal.

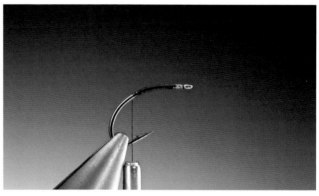

2 Run a fine foundation of tying thread about halfway along the hook shank.

3 Select a single long black barb from your chosen tail feather.

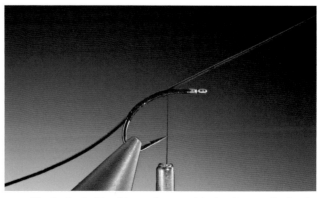

4 Tie the barb (fiber) in as shown with the tip over the hook eye and secure all the way down to the bend of the hook.

5 Trim away the excess barb over the hook eye. Attach a hackle plier and wrap the barb in tight even turns to form a segmented body. Tie off at the thorax.

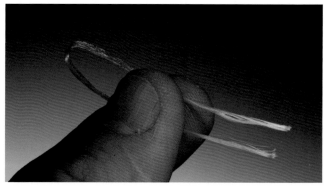

6 Take a 12cm length of your selected color of polypropylene yarn for the post, as shown.

7 Place the polypropylene loop around your tying thread and on top of the hook shank, so that the weight of your bobbin holds it in place.

8 Secure the polypropylene loop and wrap a foundation of tying thread at the base of the post, as shown. This will give a solid foundation for wrapping the hackle later.

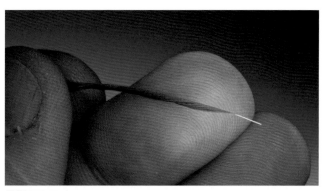

9 Prepare a saddle hackle by stripping off 5mm of the fibers from one side and 30mm of the fibers from the other.

10 Tie on your hackle as shown, with the stripped stem up the post foundation. Return your tying thread to the rear of the thorax.

11 Tie in a single ostrich herl by its butt end.

12 Wrap the ostrich herl in tight, even turns forward and tie off tight behind the hook eye.
Trim away the excess and whip finish.

13 Remove your tying thread and re-position your hook vertically in the vise, as shown.

14 Re-attach your tying thread at the base of the post, tight into the thorax.

15 Attach your hackle pliers and wrap the hackle, concave-side down, so with each turn, the hackle stem sits tight into the last, towards the thorax.
Tie off, with one turn over the hackle and one under, closer to the thorax.

16 Trim off the surplus hackle and cut the polypropylene post down to 1cm.

17 Before you make a whip finish, in between the last turn of hackle and the thorax, place a drop of varnish on the thread. Whip finish and remove your tying thread.

18 Re-position your fly in the vise.

19 Using a cauterizing tool, carefully melt the polypropylene post, taking care not to touch it with the cauterizing tip.

20 Melt the polypropylene down onto the hackle top, so that it forms a small ball. Your Para-weld Hatching Midge is now finished.

21 The small polypropylene ball works well as a quick sight indicator in low light and rough water.

26

Willow Fly

Petitjean twist and wrapping • CDC Reverse hackle winging

One of the late autumn's highlights is a great hatch of needle flies, *Leuctra,* especially here on the big grayling rivers of mid-Norway. Although the hatches begin as early as June and run until November, the climax is August and September.

These small stoneflies can be difficult to see on the best of days, especially amongst the autumn's fall of floating foliage, and remember they crawl onto land to hatch, so you will always find more on the bank than on the water. Because they hatch and mate on land, it's the females when they return to the water to lay eggs that are of the greatest interest to the fish.

In late August a few years ago, we experienced great grayling fishing on the river Glomma here in Norway. We quickly realized what was on the grayling's menu, so the greatest challenge was making a clean drift without any drag through the many differing surface currents between the rod and the feeding fish. Each different current was pulling and holding the line at different speeds. This we overcame whenever possible by presenting the fly directly into the feeding window of rising fish, keeping the drift short but effective!

The other method was to fish directly upstream while wading and using a parachute cast (a simple cast that is made by quickly dipping the tip of the rod down towards the water at the end of the cast just before the leader straightens out). This causes the line to fall in a wavy snake-like form, making mending the line as it drifts back towards you easier without drag.

I developed this pattern using a Marc Petitjean technique that he calls twist and wrap. This simple but effective CDC technique can be used for most

dry fly bodies. For larger bodies you can use two or more CDC hackles. But care must be taken that only one twist is made for each wrap of hackle.

If more twists are made, it over-stresses the delicate CDC hackle stem and may cause it to break. Making one twist after each wrap distributes the stress along the whole length of the hackle and means the stress is not concentrated at the thinnest point, as it would be when twisted whole.

You should also brush the fibers of the hackle down the stem with your finger and thumb with each wrap, so they are caught against the hook shank and give the segmented body volume.

Larger CDC hackles work best with the twist and wrap body technique.

The wing should lie tight to the body and flat. It should also extend a little further than the rear of the body. The wings on the natural are dark brown but the blue dun wing makes this pattern more visible when fishing.

This is important when fishing for grayling as the rises can be extremely difficult to see, if at all, especially when fishing a ripple, so keeping your eye on the fly is paramount.

TECHNIQUES MASTERED

- **Twist and wrap body**
  Technique for using a CDC hackle to create a very buoyant and slender CDC segmented body.

- **Reverse CDC hackle wing**
  A simplified version of the reverse hackle winging technique using a blue dun CDC hackle and a plastic tube.

- **CDC thorax and legs**
  Using a Magic Tool to spin a fine CDC dubbing brush that is used for the thorax and legs of this pattern.

You can also tie this pattern spent by adding more wings at 90 degrees to the hook shank.

When spinning the CDC for the thorax and legs, it should be a light open dubbing brush—too much CDC here will make the fly fish too high. Stoneflies lie much deeper in the surface than mayflies and caddis flies.

Tying the Willow Fly

THE DRESSING

Hook: Mustad R30 #12-16
Thread: Black
Body: Dark brown or black CDC hackle
Wing: Blue dun CDC hackle
Thorax: Dark brown or black CDC hackle

WATCH THE VIDEO

youtu.be/re78jf2I3jI
Tying the Willow Fly with Barry Orde Clarke

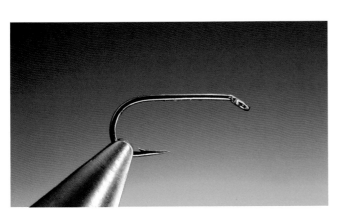

1 Secure your hook in the vise with the shank horizontal.

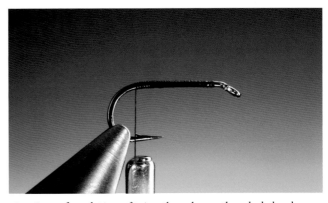

2 Lay a foundation of tying thread over the whole hook shank.

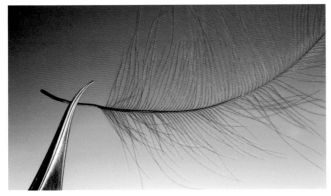

3 Select a large CDC hackle and strip off the down fibers at the base of the stem.

4 Attach the hackle stem to the hook shank with two loose turns of tying thread.

5 Pull the hackle through the tying thread loops and tighten the tying thread just as you get to the end, to catch and secure the hackle tip.

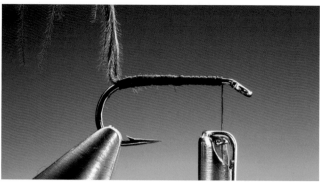

6 Wind your tying thread forward towards the hook eye and twist the CDC hackle twice so that the fibers wrap around the hackle stem. Don't try and twist any more than twice or the hackle will break!

7 With each turn of hackle make one twist to form the segmented body. When the whole hook shank is covered forward to the thorax, tie off and remove the excess hackle.

8 With straight scissors trim off all the fibers.

9 Your segmented needle fly body should now look like this.

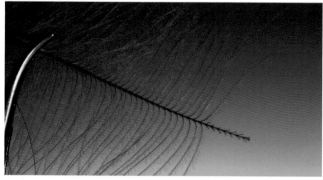

10 Select a blue dun CDC hackle and trim off the point end of the hackle as shown.

11 Take a 1cm length of a fine plastic tube-fly tube and thread it over the end of the hackle. When pulled down over the hackle this will form the wing and hold it in position ready for tying in.

12 Place the wing on top of the hook shank and secure with a few wraps of tying thread, close to the tube.

13 Secure the wing. Trim off the stripped tip of the hackle.

14 Remove the tube and trim off the excess hackle and tie down over the thorax.

15 Load a Magic Tool with only one side of a CDC hackle. You don't need much CDC for this!

16 Split your tying thread or spin the hackle in a dubbing loop, keeping the fibers as long as possible—they can always be trimmed down. Wrap the CDC hackle forward covering the thorax.

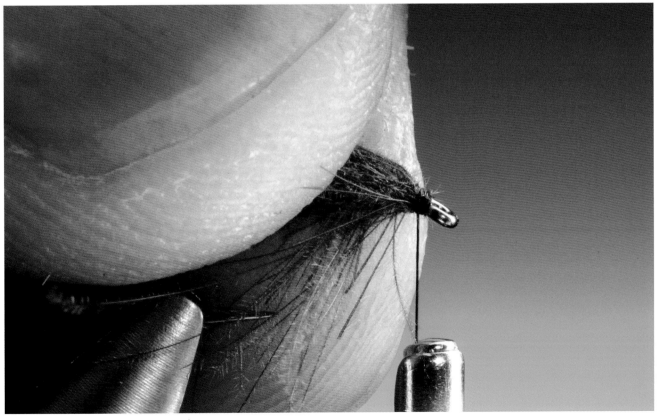

17 Holding the fibers back make a few turns of tying thread to form the head.

18 Now pull two long CDC fibers forward and tie down. Whip finish.

19 Remove the tying thread. Spin your fly upside down and trim off the CDC fibers level with the rear body on the underside. Make sure that you keep some of the side fibers for the legs and antennae.

20 Your finished CDC needle fly.

21 Underside with the segmented CDC body and the correct profile.

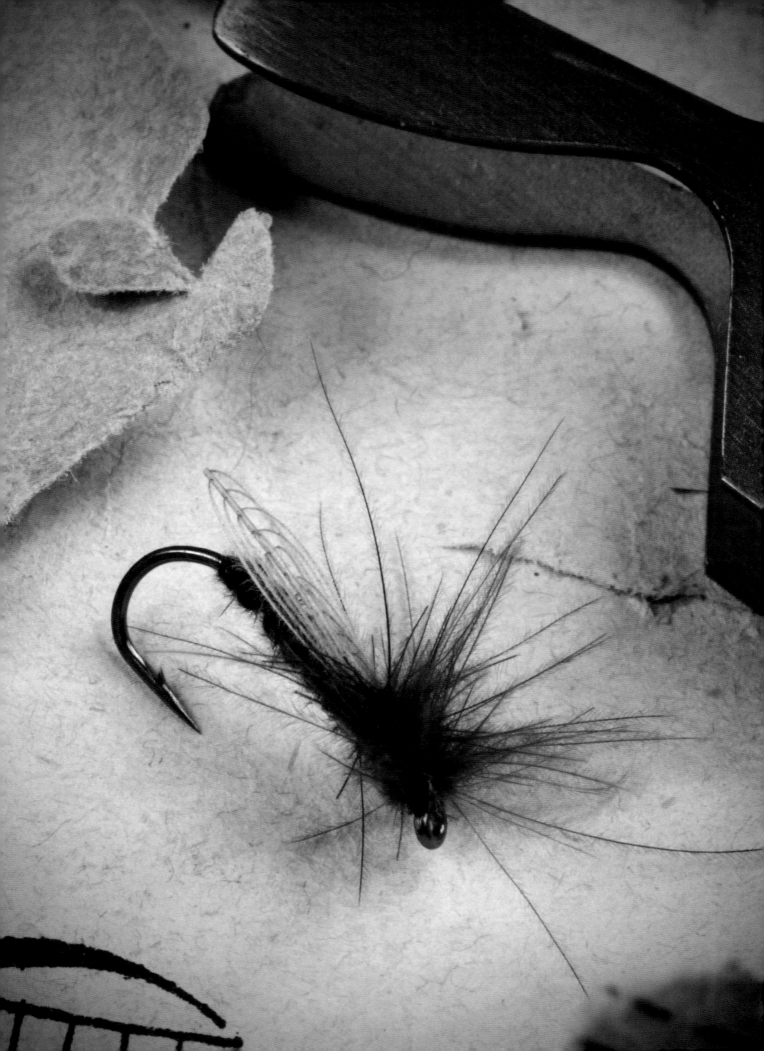

27

John Storey

Tying the forward-sloping "emerger" wing • Peacock herling

This old north country pattern has a unique appearance. The original was created in 1830 by the man of the same name, the first of three generations of riverkeepers on the Ryedale Angler's Club waters of the river Rye in North Yorkshire.

The original was a wet fly, had no wing and resembled many other trout and grayling patterns

of the time, using only peacock herl and a brown cock hackle.

It was reinvented with each generation of the family as they became riverkeepers.

It was John Storey's grandson William Arthur Storey, the last of the riverkeepers, who redesigned

his grandfather's wet fly into a dry and added the unique front-sloping wing. This could be viewed as a ground-breaking pattern.

There was method in his madness. The unique tying style was designed to present the fly as an emerger rather than a traditional dry fly of the time.

The John Storey is tied with a short, stumpy peacock herl body leaving a good deal of the hook bend visible and undressed. This pulls the fly into an upright position, the bend functioning as a 'keel'. This, coupled with the wing acting as the sail, means that the fly floats vertically, on the hackle, rather like a Klinkhamer—presenting the fly as an emerger.

I find that best quality mallard drake grey flank feathers are the best to use for a fine wing on the John Storey.

TECHNIQUES MASTERED

- **Forward-sloping wing**
  An old technique for tying a forward-sloping emerger wing using a mallard flank feather.

- **Peacock herl body**
  Technique for creating perfect traditional peacock herl bodies with a slight taper towards the rear.

- **Traditional collar hackle**
  How to prepare and wrap a dense traditional dry fly collar hackle for perfect results.

Tying the John Storey

....
THE DRESSING
....

Hook: Mustad R30 #10-16
Thread: Black
Wing: Mallard drake breast
　　　　or flank feather
Body: One or two peacock herls
Hackle: Brown cock hackle

....
WATCH THE VIDEO
....

youtu.be/BLNj0hAHPSE

Tying a John Storey dry fly with
Barry Ord Clarke

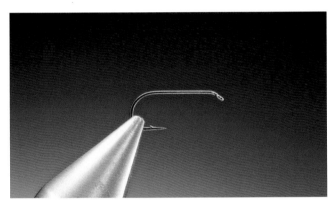

1 Secure your dry fly hook in the vise, as shown, with the hook shank horizontal.

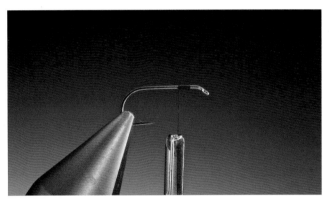

2 A little back from the hook eye, run a short foundation of tying thread along a few mm of the hook shank.

3 Select a well-marked mallard breast or flank feather for the wing.

4 Prepare the chosen feather as shown by stripping off the barbs until you get the correct wing size required.

5 Tie in the mallard wing flat, as shown, on top of the hook shank just behind the hook eye.

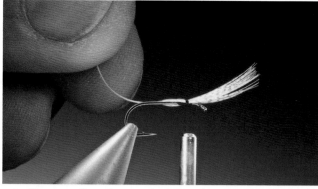

6 You can adjust the wing length and position by carefully pulling on the stem.

7 Once you are satisfied with the wing position, secure with a few turns of tying thread. Trim off the remaining stem and wind the tying thread back along the hook shank.

8 Select and tie in a nice fuzzy peacock herl, leaving a little room at the rear of the hook. Run your tying thread forward to the wing.

9 Attach a hackle plier to the peacock herl and wrap forward in tight even turns, taking care not to twist the herl as you wind forward.

10 Tie off the peacock herl, leaving enough room for the hackle. Make sure that you have a nice even foundation between the herl body and wing to wrap the hackle.

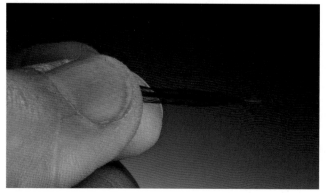

11 Select and prepare a brown cock hackle, as shown.

12 Tie in the hackle 90 degrees to the hook shank, tight into the herl body.

Continues page 244

13 Now take your time to wrap the hackle, trying to keep each turn tight into the previous one. Tie off at the wing base. Remove the excess hackle and whip finish. Place a drop or two of varnish on the head of the fly, taking care not to get any on the wing.

28

Damsel Stalking Bug

Marabou tail • Peacock herl wing casing • CDC thorax and legs

This impressionistic interpretation of a swimming damsel nymph is an ideal stalking pattern for sight fishing, but to tie it correctly, it needs attention to material, detail and proportions.

Marabou plumes originally came from the African marabou stork. These birds have been strictly protected for many years but our substitute comes almost exclusively from the thighs of the domestic turkey.

Turkey marabou is a favorite material for sub-surface patterns such as streamer wings, but it is also used extensively in patterns such as leeches, buggers and damsel and dragonfly nymphs.

The individual marabou fibers are extremely soft and mobile, producing a sinuous, lively action when fished, especially on patterns that are weighted. This gives a jigging movement which uses the marabou to full effect.

The marabou used here is not from the shorter marabou bloods or shorts as they are also known, but the larger marabou plumes, with the ultra-fine tapered barbs.

These are extra-sensitive to any movement in the water.

In order to create the correct swimming action in this attractor pattern, it's also important that you don't use too much marabou in the tail as this will reduce the animation in the jigging effect when fished.

In fact, the key to tying a successful stalking bug is all to do with the swimming action. The hook weight and style for this pattern is not random. The Mustad C67S is a 2X Heavy & 3X short hook with a straight eye, which will concentrate the weight at the very head of the pattern and induce a 'hinged' effect, where the hook finishes and the fine-tipped marabou tail begins, causing that nervous jigging action which is a real attractor factor.

Attention should be given to the length of the tail: too short and it will reduce the action; too long and it will undoubtably wrap and catch around the hook bend when casting.

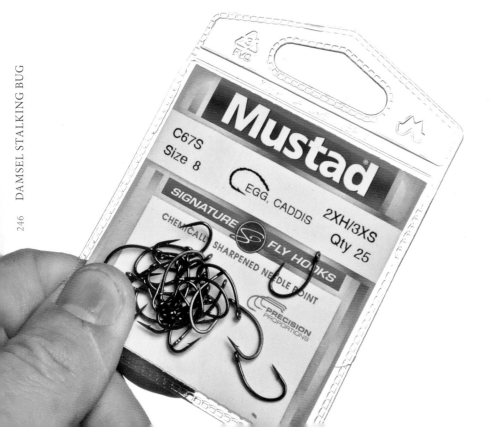

Tying the Damsel Stalking Bug

THE DRESSING

Hook: Mustad C67S #8-10
Thread: Olive
Tail: Fine olive marabou
Underbody: Lead wire
Wing case: Peacock herl
Thorax: Two olive CDC hackles

WATCH THE VIDEO

youtu.be/-B2zxeoJIyA
Tying the Damsel Stalking Bug with
Barry Ord Clarke

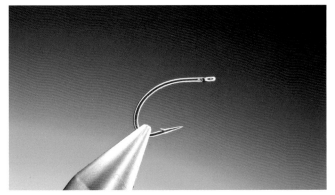

1 Secure your curved hook in the vise, as shown, with the hook shank horizontal.

2 Run a fine foundation of tying thread along two-thirds of the hook shank.

3 Select a medium bunch with fine tapered olive marabou. Here, less is more: tie in too much marabou and the swimming action will be disabled.

4 Tie down the butt ends of the marabou as shown. This will create a good foundation and give the lead wire more purchase. Return your tying thread to the base of the tail.

5   Take some lead wire, about 8cm for a size 10 hook.

6   Make eight or ten tight, neat wraps of lead wire. Make sure that you leave enough room between the lead wire and hook eye.

7   Cover the lead wire with tying thread so that it is secure and won't move. Now cut approximately eight strands of peacock herl and tie these in, on top of the hook shank, tight into the tail base.

8   Load a Petitjean Magic Clip with two or more olive CDC hackles. Make sure that the long fibers are all at the same end of the clip as shown.

9   Split your tying thread and make a CDC dubbing brush with the long CDC fibers at the base of the dubbing brush, so that when the brush is wound around the thorax, the longest fibers will finish at the hook eye.

Continued on page 250

10 Wind the CDC forward over the lead underbody and finish just behind the hook eye.

11 Take hold of the peacock herl, being careful to keep all the fibers parallel, so that they don't cross each other. Pull these over the CDC thorax and secure with a few turns of tying thread.

12 Trim off the excess peacock herl close to the hook eye. Now, starting at the hook eye, wind your tying thread back towards the wing case to cover the herl ends correctly.

13 Whip finish and remove your tying thread. From the underside of the body, give the CDC a good brushing to pull out any trapped fibers. Take care not to damage the peacock herl wing case.

14 Place a drop of varnish on the head of the fly and it's finished.

THE AUTHOR

Born in England, Barry Ord Clarke is an internationally-acclaimed fly tyer, photographer and author. He has won medals in the world's most prestigious flytying competitions, and his own flies can be seen in the iconic Flyfishers' Club collection in London and in the Catskill Master Fly Collection in the Catskill Museum in the United States.

In 2016, he was awarded the coveted Claudio D'Angelo award for Best International Fly Tyer.

In 2018, he completed seven years' work with Marc Petitjean for the book *Petitjean CDC*.

For the past twenty-five years he has lived in Norway where he works as a professional photographer and flytying consultant for Mustad, and Veniard Ltd.

You can find Barry's flytying demonstrations on his successful blog and YouTube channel, The Feather Bender.

© David Edwards

The Feather Bender flies on YouTube

To watch the YouTube videos of the tying sequences in this book you can follow any of these options:

WATCH THE VIDEO

youtu.be/p9T_oeW5enY

Tying the Mutant Melt Glue Ant with Barry Ord Clarke

1. To use the QR code: open the camera on your smartphone or chosen device. Hold the camera over the red QR code and your web browser will pop up automatically, leading you to the YouTube video of Barry tying that fly.

2. Or key in to your browser the URL (YouTube link) as shown in the book immediately beneath the "Watch the Video" heading.

3. Or type in to your web browser the full fly title as it appears at the start of each step-by-step tying section of the book. The video will come up.

Tying notes

Useful websites & organizations

54 Dean Street
www.54deanstreet.com
info@54deanstreet.com

Ahrex hooks
www.ahrexhooks.com
info@ahrexhooks.com

Bug Bond
www.bug-bond.com
David@bugbond.com

Chevron Hackles
www.chevronhackles.com
Chevronhackles@yahoo.co.uk

Cookshill Flytying Materials
www.cookshill-flytying.co.uk

Deer Creek
www.deercreek.co.uk
deercreekflies@gmail.com

Farlows
www.farlows.co.uk

Fly Box Direct
www.flyboxdirect.co.uk

Fly Only Online
www.flyonlyonline.co.uk

Fly Shack
www.flyshack.co.uk

Friends of fly fishing
www.friends-of-flyfishing.net
haas@friends-of-flyfishing.net

Fulling Mill
www.fullingmill.co.uk

Funky Flytying
www.funkyflytying.co.uk
sales@funky-products.com

Glasgow Angling Centre
www.fishingmegastore.com
sales@fishingmegastore.com

Hareline Dubbin Inc
www.hareline.com
hareline@hareline.com

John Norris of Penrith Ltd
www.johnnorris.co.uk

Lakeland Flytying
www.lakelandflytying.com

Live 4 fly fishing
http://live4flyfishing.pl/
live4flyfishing@gmail.com
info@live4flyfishing.pl

Mustad Hooks
www.mustad-fishing.com

Nature's Spirit
http://www.naturesspiritflytying.net

Orvis
www.orvis.co.uk (UK)
www.orvis.com (USA)

Partridge of Redditch
www.partridge-of-redditch.co.uk

Peak Fishing
Peakfishing.com
info@peakfishing.com

Petitjean Fishing Equipment
www.petitjean.com
info@petitjean.com

Polish Quills
www.polishquills.com
info@polishquills.com

Semperfli
www.semperfli.net

Sportfish
www.sportfish.co.uk

The Essential Fly
www.theessentialfly.com

The Flydressers' Guild
www.flydressersguild.org

The Flytying Company
www.flytyingcompany.co.uk

Trout Catchers
www.troutcatchers.co.uk

Trout Line
www.troutline.ro
office@troutline.ro

Veniard Ltd
www.veniard.com
sales@veniard.com

Virtual Nymph Products
www.virtual-nymph.com
sales@virtual-nymph.com

Wapsi Fly
www.wapsifly.com
pat@wapsifly.com

Whitetail Fly Tieing Supplies
www.whitetailflytieing.com

INDEX

INDEX